Henry Sebastian Bowden

**Guide to the Oratory, South Kensington**

with explanations and plates

Henry Sebastian Bowden

**Guide to the Oratory, South Kensington**
*with explanations and plates*

ISBN/EAN: 9783741135392

Manufactured in Europe, USA, Canada, Australia, Japa

Cover: Foto ©Thomas Meinert / pixelio.de

Manufactured and distributed by brebook publishing software
(www.brebook.com)

Henry Sebastian Bowden

**Guide to the Oratory, South Kensington**

ST. PHILIP NERI,
FOUNDER OF THE ORATORY.

# GUIDE TO.

# THE ORATORY

## SOUTH KENSINGTON

*WITH EXPLANATIONS AND PLATES*

EDITED BY

HENRY SEBASTIAN BOWDEN

PRIEST OF THE ORATORY

SEVENTH THOUSAND

LONDON
BURNS & OATES, LIMITED
1897

*Nihil obstat.*

GULIELMUS T. GORDON,

Cong. Orat.

*Imprimatur.*

✠ HERBERTUS,

Archiep. Westmonast.

*Die 30 Dec. 1892.*

# PREFACE

·

THE "Guide to the Oratory" has been compiled
to supply a descriptive account of the Church
and its contents, together with such information
regarding Catholic doctrines and devotions as is
constantly demanded by visitors.

Special thanks are due to Rev. W. Gildea, D.D.,
St. Thomas' Seminary, Hammersmith, for many
valuable suggestions and corrections ; to Rev. F.
Neville, The Oratory, Edgbaston, Birmingham, for
his permission to give the extracts quoted from
Cardinal Newman's writings ; to Messrs. Kegan
Paul, Trench, Trübner & Co., Charing Cross
Road, for the use accorded of the "Catholic
Dictionary" ; and to Messrs. Valentine and Sons,
Photographers, Dundee, for leave to reproduce

their excellent "phophyles" of the Church and its Chapels.

The notices of the Saints are taken, as a rule, from the "Miniature Lives of the Saints," which is under the same editorship as the "Guide."

H. S. B.

# ADMISSION TO THE ORATORY

THE ORATORY is open

From 6.30 A.M. to 12.30 P.M

,,   2.30 P.M.  ,,   6.30 P.M.

,,   7.20 P.M.  ,,    10 P.M.

Admission is free at all times when the Church is open, and to all the Services. A certain portion is reserved at the High Mass,

# THE SERVICES.

SUNDAYS.—Mass at 6.30, 7, 7.30, 8, 8.30, 9, 1.0 A.M.

> High Mass, 11 A.M.

> Vespers and Benediction followed by Catechism, 3.30 P.M.

> Evening Service, Confraternity, Sermon and Benediction, 7 P.M.

HOLIDAYS.—Mass and High Mass as on Sunday.

> Vespers, 4.30 P.M.

> Evening Service, Sermon and Benediction, 8 P.M.

WEEK-DAYS.—Mass, 6.30, 7, 7.30, 8, 8.30, 9, 10 A.M.

> Evening Service, 8 P.M.

BENEDICTION is given on all Greater Feasts at 8 P.M., and on Thursdays and Saturdays at 4.30 P.M. Twice daily, 4.30 P.M. and 8 P.M., through the month of May, and at 8 P.M. with the ROSARY through the month of October.

PROCESSIONS.—There are Processions of the Blessed Sacrament after the High Masses of Exposition and Deposition, Tuesday and Thursday of the fourth week in Lent ; after the High Mass of Corpus Christi ; and after Vespers on the Sunday within the Octave.

Processions of the Blessed Virgin take place on the first and last Sunday of May ; The Assumption, August 15 ; the Immaculate Conception, December 8, and the following Sunday.

PROCESSIONS WITH SERVICES FOR THE DEAD, on November 2, All Souls' Day, and the Sunday following.

CONFESSIONS are heard whenever the Church is open. The bell should be rung by St. Philip's Altar if a Confessor be not in attendance.

# TABLE OF CONTENTS.

# TABLE OF CONTENTS.

# PLATES

# LETTERPRESS ILLUSTRATIONS.

# GUIDE TO THE ORATORY.

## FOUNDATION OF THE ORATORY.

THE Church of the Oratory, situated at the junction of the Brompton, Fulham, and Cromwell Roads, derives its name from the Congregation of Secular Priests by whom it is served. The Institute was founded by St. Philip Neri in Rome in the sixteenth century, and entitled the Oratory from the little chapel of St. Girolamo della Carità where the saint began his work. By the rules of the Institute the Fathers are to lead a Community life, under obedience but without vows ; and are to give themselves to three special works, Prayer, Preaching, and the Sacraments. Prayer includes, besides the spiritual exercises of the Community, the Liturgical Services of the Church and daily popular devotions. The preaching is to be daily, and delivered in the form, for the most part, of

A

familiar instruction ; and to afford every facility in the frequentation of the Sacraments, Confessors are to be in attendance whenever the Church is open.

## THE ORATORY IN ENGLAND

In 1847, the Oratory was introduced into England by Cardinal, then Fr., Newman ; St. Philip's Institute having been selected for him and his companions during their stay in Rome, by Pius IX., then Sovereign Pontiff, as especially adapted to the needs of this country.   Their residence was first at Mary Vale near Oscott, whence, after a temporary sojourn at St. Wilfrid's, Cotton Hall, Staffordshire, they removed to Alcester Street, Birmingham, in 1849.   Later in the same year, Fr. Faber was sent by Cardinal Newman to found the London House. A site was found in 24–25 King William Street, Strand, and there the Oratory was opened in a building previously used as a whisky store, now occupied by the Charing Cross Theatre.

In the King William Street Oratory, Fr. Faber preached regularly, attracting large congregations, and his hymns, composed expressly for the Oratory night-services, now so widely known, were there first sung.   There also, in 1850, Cardinal, then Dr., Newman, delivered his lectures on Anglican

*To face p.* 3.

THE FAÇADE.

Difficulties. In October 1852 more suitable and spacious premises were found for the Oratory in its present abode in South Kensington, where the Community was transferred, and a temporary Church was opened in March 1854.

## THE NEW CHURCH, SOUTH KENSINGTON.

In 1880 plans were procured by competition for a permanent Church. The Church was to be of the Renaissance style, as being that of the Mother Church of the Oratory in Rome, and best adapted for the special work of the Oratory, the circular arch admitting of a spacious Sanctuary for the celebration of the liturgical offices, and the accommodation of a large number of persons within sight of the Altar and sound of the pulpit. There were to be not less than nine side Altars, and space was to be shown for twenty Confessionals. The design of Mr. H. Gribble was selected and executed, with the exception of the Façade and outer Dome. The Church, having been previously consecrated by Dr. Bagshawe, Bishop of Nottingham, was opened by Cardinal Manning, in the presence of the Bishops of England, on St. Mark's Day, April 24, 1884. The Façade, now in course of erection, consists of a Portico with two flanking Belfry Towers, 125 feet high.    The eastern tower serves as the Baptistery, which, according to the ritual, should be without the Church.

## THE EXTERIOR DOME.

Thanks to the generosity of an anonymous benefactor, the exterior dome was erected in 1896. Its general outline most resembles that of SS. Ambrogio and Carlo, Corso, Rome.    It is constructed of a framework of steel with wooden ribs, faced with sixty tons of lead of the finest quality.    The height from the ground line to the summit of the cross is 200 feet.    The height of the lantern, including the ball and cross, is 47 feet, of the cross itself, 6 feet.    The architect was Mr. G. Sherrin, 33, Finsbury Circus, E.C.    The whole composition effectively completes and crowns the Church of the Oratory.

## THE INTERIOR.

On entering the building by the western central door, the Nave, with a breadth 51 feet between the walls, is at once a striking feature.    It is, in fact, the widest nave in England, with the exception

From Photograph by Valentine & Sons.

THE NAVE.

To face p. 4.

of York Minster, being 10 feet wider than St. Paul's, and 15 feet in excess of that of Westminster Abbey. The order, or entablature, is carried at a height of 50 feet on twin Corinthian pilasters, with a pedestal base ; both composed of solid blocks of Devonshire marble, many of which weigh three tons each. The height of the nave to the interior vaulting is 73 feet. Intersecting the nave at its junction with the Sanctuary are two transepts of 50 feet, and between them rises the dome 53 feet in interior diameter, and about 125 feet in height from the floor level to the ceiling. The low dome was selected for the purpose of light and sound, and from the fact that its lantern is visible from a greater distance within the Church. The vaulting of both nave and dome is of concrete, a material of extreme hardness, fireproof, and for the first time, we believe, employed here in such extensive spans. Three arches between the pilasters, supported by double columns of Devonshire marble, form an opening to side chapels, 30 feet square ; the chapels being connected by a passage 6 feet wide. The fenestration is obtained by domical skylights in each bay of the nave, and by large windows above the order. The total length of the interior from the nave entrance to the Sanctuary wall is 240 feet ; the nave itself being 170 feet, and the Sanctuary 70 feet in length.

## ON CEREMONIES.

For any intelligent apprehension of the interior of a Catholic Church, or the services conducted there, it must be remembered that Catholicism is essentially a ceremonial religion. Holy Water, Images, Pictures, Lights, Music, Incense, the least sign, movement, or word employed in the devotions, ritual and liturgy, have their appointed significance. A preliminary explanation of ceremonies, their nature and purpose, seems therefore expedient.

The word ceremony, taken in a wide sense, signifies any outward act used in the worship of God. That exterior signs are suitably employed in the worship of God by man, mere reason suffices to prove. We are not pure spirits, but spirit and matter, or body and soul; and we naturally therefore express by outward acts our interior thought or feeling. Then again, just as we naturally manifest our thoughts and feelings by external actions, so also it is by the action of external things upon our senses that thoughts and feelings are excited within us. It is, then, in strict accordance with our nature that appeal should be made to our religious instincts through the medium of sensible representations.

Lastly, though God has no need of these outward signs to learn our inward dispositions, as both body and soul come from Him, and depend for existence on Him, it is only fitting that both should be used in His service.

Ceremonies or ceremonial are, then, essential to religion, and no creed which has professed to dispense with them has ever gained acceptance, or had more than an ephemeral existence. But since these outward acts are the expression of our faith in God, they ought to be of such a kind as to indicate the truth which they are intended to signify, and to do this with all becoming reverence. Legitimate authority must therefore watch over and regulate their use. Employed without proper sanction, signs and postures may easily become a puerile and senseless mimicry; and the most sacred words a profane and grotesque expression of hysterical emotion. To guard against these evils, we find that, from the first, God Himself ordained the manner of Divine worship. He prescribed the victim for Abraham's sacrifice, and the sign of the covenant which was to follow (Genesis xxvii. *passim*). He vouchsafed a vision to Jacob that he might set up a stone with the title, " The House of God " (Genesis xxviii. 11). The Law He delivered to Israel consisted in great part of the ceremonial to be observed in every relation of civil and family life, above all in the Tabernacle worship; and for the Temple itself, its very materials, vessels, rites, sacrifices, priesthood, were divinely appointed. So too, when Christ came, and with Him and through Him the fulness of grace and truth, He Himself determined the material and sensible signs by which the salvation He purchased for us was to be conveyed to the souls of men. He appointed what is essential to the Christian religion, the matter and form of the Sacraments : thus, Water and the words to be used for Baptism ; Bread and Wine with the consecrating form for the Holy Eucharist. What is non-essential, the ceremonies which are to accompany the administration of the Sacraments and the proper order of Divine worship, He has left to His Church to determine. To her belongs, as St. Paul says, "to put all things in order "; and any notable departure from her ritual, or any serious innovation therein, is a grave sin. With what consistency and uniformity her ritual and ceremonial has been governed, ancient monuments still in existence declare. The Catacombs reveal to us in stone, metal, and colour, the Faith and Worship of the early Church. There we find Altars, Crosses, Pictures, Images, Relics, representations of Purgatory, Vessels, Vestments, Holy Water, Incense, the appointments and ritual of the Church of to-day. And

this is so, because while all preceding rites, Patri-
archal and Mosaic, led up to, and were fulfilled in,
the Christian Dispensation, that Dispensation alone
endures, as containing the substance and reality of
Him, who is " yesterday, to-day, the same for
ever."

For us as Christians only one further change
remains.   Our ceremonies, says St. Thomas,
signify grace already won, and regard the future
only so far as they typify Heaven.   The Blessed
" in patria " have nothing more to hope, for their
every desire is fulfilled.   With them, therefore,
there are no figures or symbols, but only Thanksgiving and the Voice of Praise ; and hence St.
John, when he speaks ot the City of the Blessed,
says, " 1 saw no Temple therein, for the Lord God
Almighty is the Temple thereof, and the Lamb "
(Apoc. vii. 14).


## HOLY WATER.

At the entrance door are two standard Holy
Water basins of Italian design.   Water is a natural
symbol of interior purity :   " I will pour out
clean water upon you," God says by the Prophet
Ezechiel (chap. xxvii. v. 25), "and you shall be
clean " ; and the ceremony of aspersion, expressing

the cleansing of the soul, needed for the Divine
worship, is prescribed by the Mosaic law.  A

HOLY WATER BASIN.

laver stood before the Tabernacle, that the priests
might wash their hands before offering sacrifice.
Exodus ch. xxx., and Numbers ch. xix., gives
detailed instructions concerning " the water of
aspersion," and the mode of sprinkling.  This rite
of ablution is one of the many ordinances of the
old law engrafted on the ritual of the Church.
The antiquity of the usage is testified by the

marble or terra-cotta vessels for Holy water still preserved in the Catacombs. In the second century Tertullian informs us that it was the custom to wash the hands and face before entering the House of God ; and in the ninth century this custom was a recognised ecclesiastical ceremony. Before High Mass on all Sundays the celebrant blesses the congregation with Holy Water, while the verse "Asperges me" (Ps. l. 9), or in Paschal time the "Vidi aquam" (Ezech. xlvii. 1), is being sung ; both texts symbolising contrition for sin, and hope of pardon. "Holy Water," says the Catholic Dictionary, "is therefore placed at the doors of the Church, that the faithful at all times may sign themselves with it as they enter, accompanying the outward rite with the inward act of sorrow and love." The ceremony and prayers used in blessing the Holy Water will further explain its significance. "Water and salt are exorcised, and so withdrawn from the power of Satan, by whom, since the fall, even inanimate things have been corrupted and abused. Prayers are said, that the water and salt may promote the spiritual and temporal health of those to whom they are applied ; finally, the water and salt are mingled together with the sign of the Cross, in the name of the Holy Trinity." The water, being thus solemnly blessed, if used with proper disposi-

tions of contrition and charity, becomes a special
means of grace, by the prayer of the Church taking
effect at the time of its application." ("Catholic
Dictionary," art. "Holy Water.")


## CHAPEL OF THE SACRED HEART.

Beginning our circuit by the western aisle, the
first Chapel is that of the Sacred Heart. The
Altar of this Chapel is designed much on the lines
of that in the Chapel of the Scuola di San Giovanni,
Venice. The frontal is composed of two panels of
African marble on a ground of pale Siena, enclosing a centre of red African in white statuary
mouldings. The four pilasters supporting the
entablature are of white Sicilian, enriched with
flutings of red Languedoc and Arabesque carvings.
The three niches are lined with green Campan,
the bases and shells being of Siena and the
frieze of Griotte. Within the central niche stands
a statue in Carrara marble, representing the Sacred
Heart. The floor and rails, rich in Paonazzo and
other marbles, are a votive offering in memory of
Louisa Edith Ward, 1895. The devotion to the
Sacred Heart of Our Lord is founded on the
fundamental doctrine of Christian faith that Christ,
being God and Man, His human nature is, by reason
of its personal union with the Eternal Word, an

CHAPEL OF THE SACRED HEART.

*To face p.* 12.

object of Divine worship.   The wise men adored the Infant Jesus in the Cave (Matt. ii. 11); the blind man when sight was given to him, falling down, adored Christ (John ix. 38); and St. Thomas, after touching the Sacred Wounds, confessed his faith in the words, "My Lord and My God" (John xx. 28).   And thus, too, the Church worships the Heart of Jesus as the Heart of God, the Divine Person to whom it is hypostatically united.

## SPREAD OF THE DEVOTION.

Since worship is the expression of faith, it is only natural to expect that when any dogma is attacked the faithful should give public expression to their faith in the doctrine assailed; in this manner they proclaim at once their protest and their desire to offer expiation for the outrage offered to God's revelation.   Thus, when the Albigenses denied the reality of the Incarnation, the devotion of the Rosary reaffirmed, by the voice of the faithful, the principal mysteries of the Life, Death, and Resurrection of Jesus Christ.   Thus, too, the Feast of Corpus Christi publicly proclaimed the doctrine of the Real Presence in opposition to the heresy of the fallen monk Berengarius; and in these later times, when Jansenius—after the example of Calvin— denied that Christ died for all men, or that all

could be saved, the devotion to the Sacred Heart
as the symbol of Christ's infinite love, reaffirmed
the Catholic doctrine that Christ's Sacrifice was
not only infinite itself, but was offered for the
whole world ; and that therefore no one is lost
but by his own perverse will.   The ends of this
devotion, then, are first : to make a return to our
Lord for His infinite love as displayed in His
Sacred Passion, and in the institution of the Holy
Eucharist.   Secondly, to offer reparation for the
insults He receives in His Sacramental Life ; and
thirdly, to obtain for ourselves an increase of the
spirit of divine love and self-sacrifice.

The devotion to the Sacred Heart, in its present
form, owes its origin to a revelation made to the
Blessed Margaret Mary Alacoque, a French Visitation Nun, in the latter part of the seventeenth
century.   It was first preached in England by her
director, the B. Paul de la Colombière, S.J., who
was sent to the Court of St. James as Confessor to
the Duchess of York.   At the breaking out of the
Titus Oates plot two years later, P. de la Colombière was first imprisoned and then banished by
Parliament.   His connection with the House of
Stuart then ceased, but the seed he had sown bore
fruit, for the first petition for a Mass in honour of
the Sacred Heart was made by Mary of Modena,
England's exiled Queen.   The first Altar erected

*To face p. 15.*

CHAPEL OF ST. JOSEPH.

in honour of the Sacred Heart in England was that of a private Chapel at Old Oscott or Mary Vale, where Dr. Milner used to say Mass.

The pictures on either side of the Altar are of the Venetian School, and represent the Circumcision of our Blessed Lord and His Presentation in the Temple.

## CHAPEL OF ST. JOSEPH.

Next to the Sacred Heart is the Chapel of St. Joseph. This is the largest of the side Chapels, owing to the addition of an apse, of sufficient size to accommodate the Altar and rails. The decoration of the apse is by Mr. J. Cosgreave and Signor Codina Langlin. The Altar, which stood in the former Oratory, is composed principally of Derbyshire alabaster, and was designed by Mr. Scoles, the architect of the Oratory House and of the Jesuits' Church, Farm Street. The domical tabernacle is a perfect architectural model. Above the Altar is a statue of St. Joseph in white marble by a Belgian artist. The Chapel is surmounted by a panelled cupola, supported on four pendentives. The pictures on either side of the Altar are of St. Philip Neri, and of St. Catherine Ricci, the Dominicaness, a friend and contemporary of the Saint.

## ST. JOSEPH.

A very special devotion is paid by the Church
to St. Joseph. Though comparatively of modern
origin, it is based on the first principle of Catholic
worship : viz., that those who are nearest to God,
should be most honoured by His Church. Now
the dignities conferred on St. Joseph were personal
and unshared by any Saint. He was chosen to
be the Spouse of the Virgin Mother of God, and
the Foster-father and Guardian of the Incarnate
Word. "Joseph," says the Holy Scripture, "was
a just man ; he was innocent and pure, as became
the husband of Mary ; he was gentle and tender,
as one worthy to be named the Father of Jesus ;
he was prudent and a lover of silence, as became
the master of the holy house ; above all, he was
faithful and obedient to Divine calls. His con-
versation was with angels rather than with men.
When he learnt that Mary bore within her womb
the Lord of Heaven, he feared to take her as his
wife, but an angel bade him fear not, and all
doubts vanished. When Herod sought the life of
the Divine Infant, an angel told Joseph in a dream
to fly with the Child and His Mother into Egypt.
Joseph at once arose, and obeyed. When the
danger was past, a third time the angel spoke, and

*To face p.* 17.

ALTAR OF THE SEVEN DOLOURS.

at his bidding the faithful Joseph returned to the peace of Nazareth.   Here for long years he lived, uniting with his domestic care and daily toil the continued contemplation of heavenly things, until his work was done, and the greatest of God's Saints breathed his last breath in the arms of Jesus and Mary."

On account of these great dignities and privileges, Pius IX., in 1871, declared St. Joseph, Patron of the Universal Church, and its Protector in its many necessities, and accorded to him the highest honour, after the Blessed Virgin.   At the same time as the Foster-father of Jesus, and the Head of the Holy Family, St. Joseph is adopted as the Guardian and model of every Christian home.


## CHAPEL OF THE SEVEN DOLOURS.

We now reach the Chapel of the Seven Dolours, again slightly varied from the others by its two quadrants, within which stands the Altar of black and white marble.   It was designed by Mr. Gribble and is intentionally severe in colouring and composition, to harmonise with its subject.   A memorial tablet on the Gospel side states that the Altar was erected by Flora, Duchess of Norfolk, who died in 1887 : " To the Mother of

Sorrows, that they who mourn may be comforted."
A companion tablet on the Epistle side bears the
text, "And God shall wipe away all tears from their
eyes" (Apoc. vii. 17). The Altar-piece picture is
of the Mater Dolorosa ; the seven swords transfix-
ing her heart represent her Seven Dolours. In the
lunette · above is a copy of the Entombment, now
in the National Gallery, by Francia (Francesco
Raibolini) of the Bolognese school (1450–1517).

## THE SEVEN DOLOURS.

The devotion of the Seven Dolours commemorates
the sufferings of the Mother of God and her supernatural constancy under them. The prophecy of
Simeon, that a sword should pierce Mary's soul,
was most perfectly fulfilled when she stood, as St.
John writes, under the Cross, and her "Compassion,"
or part in the Passion of Christ, has ever been
dwelt on by the Saints, and made the subject of
devout comment, especially by SS. Ambrose and
Bernard. The sublime Sequence of the "Stabat
Mater," composed by Jacopone dei Todi, the
Franciscan recluse, in the thirteenth century, un-
surpassed for simplicity and pathos, has done much,
says Ozanam, to kindle this devotion among the
poor and simple folk in Italy who loved its cadence

and rhythm, and knew it by heart. In the thirteenth century also, the Order of Servites, or Servants of Mary, was founded, especially in honour of the Seven Dolours. They are thus enumerated: The Prophecy of Simeon; the Flight into Egypt; the Loss of Jesus for three days; the carrying of the Cross; the Crucifixion; the Descent from the Cross; and the Entombment. The Feast of the Seven Dolours was instituted at a Provincial Council at Cologne, in 1423, in reparation for the sacrileges committed at that time by the Hussites, in their fanatical destruction of crucifixes and of the images of the Mother of Sorrows. Benedict XIII., in 1725, appointed Friday after Passion Sunday for the celebration of this feast; and, in 1814, Pius VII. directed that a second Feast of the Dolours should be kept on the third Sunday of September ("Cath. Dict.": Benedict XIV. de Festis).

In the central panels of either quadrant are mosaics of the Angels of the Passion, after Luini; in memory of John Davey, who died 1883, and Eliza Davey, who died 1874.


## ST. SEBASTIAN.

Over the northern doorway is a picture of St. Sebastian, attributed to one of the Caracci.

"St. Sebastian was an officer in the Roman army, esteemed even by the heathen as a good soldier, and honoured by the Church ever since as a champion of Jesus Christ. St. Ambrose and St. Charles Borromeo were specially devout to him; and it was while he watched and prayed in the catacombs of St. Sebastian, that St. Philip Neri received the miraculous gifts of the Holy Ghost. Born at Narbonne, Sebastian came to Rome about the year A.D. 284, and entered the lists with the powers of evil. He found the twin brothers, Marcus and Marcellinus, in prison for the faith, and when they were near yielding to the entreaties of their relatives, encouraged them to despise flesh and blood and to die for Christ. God confirmed his words by miracle; light shone around him while he spoke, he cured the sick by his prayers, and in this divine strength he led multitudes to the faith. He saw his disciples die before him, and one of them came back from heaven to tell him his own end was near. He was led before Diocletian, and at the Emperor's command, pierced with arrows, and left for dead. But God raised him up again, and of his own accord he went before the Emperor, and conjured him to stay the persecution of the Church. Again sentenced, he was at last beaten to death by clubs, and crowned his labours by the merit of a double martyrdom."

To face p. 21.

ALTAR OF ST. PHILIP.

## CHAPEL OF ST. PHILIP.

The western Transept, into which we now enter, contains the Altar of St. Philip Neri, the Founder of the Oratory. He was born at Florence, 1515; but Rome was the scene of his labours, and there he lived and worked for sixty years. Through a singular persuasiveness, the fruit both of nature and grace, he converted the worst sinners, taught the poor and simple to pray, trained men and women to be saints in their own home, and he is still known as "the Apostle of Rome." The Oratory was his chief work and the chosen weapon of his apostolate. Gathering round him men of every age and class, but principally the young, he renewed their fervour in a time of general laxity, and "showed them the more perfect way." The meetings of his disciples, held first in his own little room, then in the Oratory at San Girolamo della Carità, were transferred, as the number of his disciples increased, to St. John of the Florentines, and finally to the Vallicella. There St. Philip built his new Church, and from among his sons who were in Holy Orders, planted his Congregation of Secular Priests, known as "Fathers of the Oratory," which was approved by Gregory XIII.,

1575. Among the Saint's most famous disciples were B. Juvenal Ancina, Bishop of Saluzzo ; Baronius, the writer of the Ecclesiastical Annals ; and Palestrina, the great composer. St. Ignatius, the Founder of the Society of Jesus ; St. Charles Borromeo ; St. Camillus of Lellis, the Founder of the order for the visitation of the sick ; St. Felix of Cantalice, the Capuchin lay-brother ; St. Francis of Sales ; St. Catherine of Ricci, claimed it as an honour to be counted among his friends. The following lines on St. Philip are by Cardinal Newman :

> *I know him by his head of snow,*
> *His ready smile, his keen full eye,*
> *His words which kindle as they flow,*
> *Save he be rapt in ecstasy.*
>
> *He lifts his hands, there issues forth*
> *A fragrance virginal and rare,*
> *And now he ventures to our North*
> *Where hearts are frozen as the air.*
>
> *He comes by grace of his address,*
> *By the sweet music of his face,*
> *And his low tones of tenderness,*
> *To melt a noble, stubborn race.*
>
> *O sainted Philip, Father dear,*
> *Look on thy little ones, that we*
> *Thy loveliness may copy here,*
> *And in the eternal kingdom see.*
>
> VERSES ON VARIOUS OCCASIONS.

The Altar is composed of choice Italian and other marbles. The central panels are of Broccatello, framed in Grecian green and black marble. On either side of the Altar are two quadrant wings, surmounted by a balustrade of Paonazzo marble, on bases of Rosso antico. This arrangement, besides giving depth to the Altar-piece, serves to screen the doors, which, on either side of the transept, communicate with the house. Above the Altar, four columns in Languedoc support a large superstructure which rises to the height of the order. Within the pediment is an alto-relievo, by Moneta, a Milanese artist, of the last moments of St. Philip, with the Community kneeling round him, and Baronius, then Superior, recommending his soul. The armorial bearings on the front panels of the quadrants are those of Henry, Duke of Norfolk, the donor. The five pendant silver lamps in front of the Altar are a votive offering in memory of Lord Alexander Gordon Lennox, who died 1892.

## PORTRAITS OF ST. PHILIP.

The picture over the Altar is a copy of a contemporary portrait of St. Philip, by Guido Reni, the original of which is in the Saint's room at the Vallicella. " Art has contributed much to perpetuate the memory of the Saint. Barroccio has left a likeness of him as a boy known as 'Pippo

Buono,' and which has about it," says Capecelatro, "the air and fragrance of Paradise. Pomerancio decorated the Saint's room, when it was made into a chapel, with scenes from his life; and in the same chapel is a noble portrait of the Saint in ecstasy while saying Mass, with the server peeping cautiously in to see whether he dare enter. The vault of the apse of the Vallicella is painted in fresco by the same artist; the Saint is invoking our Blessed Lady, who is advancing to sustain the falling roof of the older Church. Guercino, who was one of the glories of the Bolognese school, left at the Vallicella a striking portrait of St. Philip. Giordano often painted our Saint, and always with the hand of a master; his noblest representation of him, all glorious in heaven and surrounded with angels, is on the ceiling of the sacristy of the Girolamini; and the chapel of St. Philip in the same church was adorned by Solimene with incidents from the Saint's life."

"The noblest work of sculpture which bears the name of the new Apostle of Rome is his colossal statue by Algardi, in the sacristy of the Vallicella. The marble glows with life, and well expresses the blended greatness and tenderness of the Saint. Thus Christian art delighted to honour the memory of the humble Saint who loved it so well, and who had such trust in its power for good" ("Life of St. Philip," vol. ii. 474).

## Relic of St. Philip.

SILVER BUST WITH RELIC OF ST. PHILIP.

On Tuesdays a wax figure, in a recumbent pos-
ture, clad in sacred vestments and containing a

relic of his body, is exposed under the Altar; and on
Tuesdays and Fridays at twelve o'clock, the blessing
of the Relic is given.   The Church honours the
relics of the Saints, because the body of every
baptized Christian, and still more of every Saint,
is sanctified by grace as the temple of the Holy
Ghost, co-operates with the soul in its earthly
conflict, and will be raised up again and reunited
to the soul at the time of the soul's final triumph.
Holy Scripture records many instances of miracles
wrought by means of relics—a proof of the divine
approval of the honour paid to these sacred remains.
With the mantle of Elias, Eliseus divided the waters
of the Jordan (4 Kings ii. 14).   The bones of
Eliseus raised a dead man to life (4 Kings xiii.
21).   The handkerchief of St. Paul cured the sick
and freed the possessed (Acts xix. 11).   And ever
since the Apostle's age the unbroken tradition of
two thousand years attests that a similar power
has been constantly exercised by the relics of God's
servants.   With regard to St. Philip, evidence was
given at his canonisation of two hundred miracles,
almost all of healing, operated through his intercession and by contact with what had been his.   And
as the Church of Antioch guarded as a peculiar
treasure the relics of St. Ignatius, and the Christians of Smyrna "preserved the bones and heart of
St. Polycarp as more precious than the richest

To face p. 20.

ALTAR WITH PICTURE OF B. SEBASTIAN VALFRE.

jeweis or gold," so do the children of St. Philip venerate as their most sacred heirloom whatever has belonged to their Father in God.

*The Fathers are in dust, yet live to God ;*
  *So says the Truth ; as if the motionless clay*
*Still held the seeds of life beneath the sod,*
  *Smouldering and struggling till the judgment-day.*

*And hence we learn with reverence to esteem*
  *Of these frail houses, though the grave confines ;*
*Sophist may urge his cunning tests, and deem*
  *That they are earth ; but they are heavenly shrines."*
    NEWMAN : " VERSES ON VARIOUS OCCASIONS."

The pictures on the left and right of the Altar are by Guercino, of St. Matthew and St. John. They were formerly in the Strutt collection, then in that of Hadzor House—Captain Galton—by whom they were presented to the Oratory.

## B. SEBASTIAN VALFRÉ.

The Altar of Languedoc and Siena with twisted columns and pediment of black marble on the northern side of St. Philip's transept, contains a picture of the B. Sebastian Valfré. He was born of poor parents at Verduno in Piedmont, 1629. He persevered, through many and great obstacles, in studying for the priesthood ; and in

1651, being then deacon, was admitted into the Oratory of Turin, at that time struggling into existence. Of this Oratory Sebastian was co-founder, and there for more than sixty years he laboured for God and for souls, with a zeal, a patience, a prudence, and a charity which made men call him a second St. Philip, the St. Philip of Turin. He changed the face of the city, protected it in war with his counsels and his prayers, and warded off from it the assaults of heresy. In his incessant labours he maintained an unbroken union of soul with God, and was preserved amid all honours, by his profound humility, and his perfect detachment from the world and from self. He refused the Archbishopric of Turin, withdrew himself, as far as possible, from all positions of dignity and influence, and strove in every way to lessen the universal veneration in which he was held. His charity was inexhaustible, and his intense love of souls softened the hardest hearts. "The slow fever," as he called his life in the Oratory, was closed by a painful but most holy death, January 30, 1710.

## B. JUVENAL ANCINA.

The portrait in crayon of a Bishop between the pilasters, adjoining the picture of the B. Sebastian,

is of the B. Juvenal Ancina.   He was a physician
in Turin.   One day, the " Dies Irae," sung at a
Requiem, revealed to him the vanity of earthly
things, and he went to Rome to seek a more
perfect life.   While in doubt as to his future, he
entered the Church of the Oratory and made the
acquaintance of St. Philip, by whose advice he entered the Congregation in 1568, being then thirty-
three.   His first care was to acquire thoroughly
the spirit of the Institute, to follow in all things
the common way, and to be a burden to none.   By
these means he became universally loved.   In
1586 he was sent to Naples to help the newly
founded Community.   He laboured there un-
weariedly for ten years, exerting himself especially
in favour of young men, whom he won in numbers
to God.   In 1596, the promotion of Baronius to
the Cardinalate led to his recall to Rome ; and in
1597, Clement VIII. named him to the See of
Saluzzo in Piedmont, then devastated by the Swiss
heretics.   Ancina fled from Rome, and protested in
every way against his elevation, but procured only
a delay ; and in 1602 he was consecrated Bishop
with his intimate friend St. Francis of Sales.   After
one year of his pastoral rule, Saluzzo became again
Catholic in faith and morals.   But the Bishop's
zeal made him enemies : a monk, whom he had
reproved for his scandalous life, found means to
administer to him a poisoned drink in the refectory.

He died in a few hours, surrounded by his Chapter,
August 31 ("Miniature Lives of the Saints,"
August 31, 1604). On February 9, 1890, the
venerable John Juvenal Ancina was solemnly beati-
fied in the large hall over the porch of the Vatican
Basilica by Leo XIII. A Triduo in honour of the
new Beatus was held at the London Oratory in
June 1890.


## THE SANCTUARY.

The Sanctuary, 50 feet wide, and 75 feet in
length from the rails to central wall of the apse,
contains the Altar of the Blessed Sacrament, which
is always reserved at the High Altar in Churches
of the Oratory; a genuflection therefore is always
made on passing this Altar and special reverence
is observed before it. The floor is composed of
inlaid wood—cinnamon, tulip, pear, mahogany,
walnut, and oak, and with the Stalls, which are of a
Renaissance Sienese model inlaid with ivory, was a
gift from Anne, Dowager Duchess of Argyll. The
altar-rails are of Sicilian, the balustrade and plinth
of Siena marble, the three gates are of metal gilt,
the walls are of foreign marbles, the ground is
Languedoc, of which material some 1600 feet are
here employed; on either side are recesses 20 fcet

To face p. 30.

THE SANCTUARY AND HIGH ALTAR.

in width, their inlaid pilasters are of jasper and onyx surmounted by gilded arches; the four projecting pilasters of the apse are of Paonazzo; the flanking panels are of jasper and onyx with statuary mouldings in relief. The onyx panels in gilt frames enclosing the central picture, are from designs on the Confession of St. Peter's. The High Altar is of statuary marble, enriched with gilt ornamentation. The gilt pendant canopy or Baldachino is copied from that suspended in the Shrine of St. Antony at Padua.

STALLS—SANCTUARY.

The central picture, representing St. Philip, the Blessed Virgin, and the Eternal Father, is by Father Philpin de Rivière, of the London Oratory, after a design by Sebastian Concha of Turin. Above the picture a cartouche, bearing a gilt heart surrounded by rays, breaks the entablature and adds much to the height of the Altar-piece. The heart represents the title of the Church, which is dedicated to the Immaculate Heart of Mary. The two angels on either side are of a good period of Italian work, and were given by the late Sir Edgar Boehm, the well-known sculptor. The picture in the western arch, 13 feet wide by 22 feet high, represents the Ponte St. Angelo in Rome, with St. Philip and the Students of the English College, who were accustomed to seek the blessing of the aged Saint before departing on their mission. The figure in red is Cardinal Allen, the founder and protector of the College ; in the background is faintly delineated the Tower of London, where so many whom St. Philip blessed won the martyr's palm. "Salvete flores martyrum," was the Saint's salutation of these youthful champions of the faith. A tradition says (Simpson's "Life of B. Edmund Campion") that the only one among them who failed to repair to St. Philip, lost heart in the conflict, and apostatised. The corresponding picture on the eastern side is the Capuchins' vision of St. Philip conducting his disciples to Paradise, related in Bacci's Life of the Saint.

The Sanctuary roof is ornamented with gilt bas-reliefs on a blue ground, those in the pendentives are modelled from the Certosa of Pavia. On either side of the windows are heroic figures of the four Evangelists. SS. Matthew and Mark occupy the western, SS. Luke and John the eastern side. The frieze and moulding of the entablature, alike of gold mosaic, bear inscribed in blue block letters the text : "Domus mea Domus orationis vocabitur, dicit Dominus," "My House shall be called a House of Prayer, saith the Lord." The decoration of the Sanctuary was designed entirely by Mr. J. Cosgreave. The large pictures in the side arches are by Mr. Codina Langlin.

## THE USE OF LIGHTS.

The twin pair of seven-branched Lamps are copied from those in the Arch of Titus, taken from the Temple of Jerusalem. The marble stands bear the arms of the Marquis of Bute, the donor. The usage of lamps and lights in Divine worship dates from earliest times, and is another instance of the Mosaic ritual finding its complete significance in the Christian Church. We read in the Acts of the Apostles (xx. 7) of the great number of lamps which burned in the upper chamber, while St. Paul continued his speech till midnight. From the first ages it was a devout custom with Christians to offer the oil and wax needed for the

c

lights of the Sanctuary. As the offering might be received from none but the faithful, its acceptance was regarded as a pledge of Church Communion. By a decree of the Congregation of Rites (22nd August 1699), an oil lamp must be always kept burning before the Altar of the Blessed Sacrament. The lamp bespeaks the Eucharistic Presence of the God-Man, who is both our light in the darkness of this world, and the pledge of our future glory. During the Triduo of the Passion, · from Holy Thursday to the morning of Holy Saturday, when the Blessed Sacrament is no longer reserved, nor the Sacrifice of the Mass offered, all the lamps in the Church are extinguished, and are only relit in the Office of Holy Saturday from the newly blessed light of the Paschal Candle, which is the symbol of the Resurrection. Lamps are burned at the other Altars, but that before the Blessed Sacrament can be always distinguished by the greater number of lights and by the veil covering the Tabernacle.

LAMP AT SIDE ALTAR.

The candles of the Altar are also of strict ritual necessity. Two lighted candles are indispensable whenever Low Mass is celebrated; six are required

for a High Mass ; twelve, at least, for Benediction
of the Blessed Sacrament. The candles must be
of pure wax and of white colour, except in the
Masses for the Dead, when candles of yellow wax
are prescribed.

It often happens that the earliest evidence for
the existence of any doctrine or ritual is furnished
by the attack of heretical opponents. Thus we
find the use of candles defended by St. Jerome in
the fourth century against the ridicule of Vigi-
lantius. The use of lights in Divine worship is
also referred to by two Christian poets, contemporaries of the great Latin Doctor. St. Paulinus
writes :

> *Above those altars bright,*
> *Like coronets of light,*
>   *The clustered lamps are hung ;*
> *And waxen tapers gleam,*
> *While from each starry beam*
>   *A fragrance wide is flung.*
>
> *By day, by night, they show*
> *So bright, 'twould seem as though*
>   *Each night were brilliant day,*
> *And day itself assumed*
> *A glory new, illumed*
>   *Afresh with heaven-sent ray.*
>                     NAT. III. S. FELICIS.

Again, Prudentius, in his well-known description
of the Martyrdom of St. Lawrence, thus describes
the Holy Sacrifice :

*In silver chalices, 'tis said,*
*Fuming the sacred blood is shed;*
*And fixed on gold, the tapers' light*
*Illumes their midnight solemn rite.*
                    LIBER PERISTEPHANON, Hymn ii. 69.

Candles are also burnt for private devotion at
the various altars, as a votive offering in honour of
the Saint invoked, and as a sign of spiritual joy
and thanksgiving; just as in the world illuminations
are a natural symbol of some special festivity or
triumph.


## THE BLESSED SACRAMENT.

The Catholic Church teaches that in the ever
Blessed Sacrament of the Altar, the Body and Blood
of Jesus Christ, together with His Soul and Divinity,
are truly, really, and substantially present on the
Altar under the appearance of bread and wine.
The motive for accepting this, as other doctrines
of faith, is the teaching of God as proposed by the
Church.   We do not purpose to set forth here the
Scriptural testimony to this truth, or the unbroken
tradition in its favour as shown by every ancient
Liturgy, but would rather call attention to the place
and importance which the doctrine holds in the
history of revelation.

In all ages, every religion, whatever its form, has

expressed one paramount desire, the reunion of man with God, the resumption in some way of that intimacy with Him, of which all primal traditions spoke. Idolatry and polytheism, magic and false spiritualism, in their myriad and fantastic forms, ancient and modern, are only a perverted endeavour to find Him, whom, ever since the fall, man by his own effort has sought in vain. For though reason does indeed tell man plainly of his Creator's existence and sovereign rights, so that all ignorance of the truth is wilful and inexcusable, yet the supernatural knowledge of God, and intimate union and friendship with Him possessed before the fall, were forfeited by Adam, not for himself alone, but for the entire human race which he represented. And thus man enters the world not as the friend of God, but as one who has forfeited God's friendship.

MONSTRANCE FOR THE BLESSED SACRAMENT.

But God wills all men to be saved, and to come to the knowledge of His truth, and therefore to all who seek Him, He gives grace and faith sufficient

for salvation. Moreover, in addition to revealing
Himself to the mind and heart within, God has
constantly made Himself known, in some external
manner and by means of types and figures fore-
shadowed with ever-increasing distinctness, that
supreme external manifestation of Himself, the
great mystery of the Incarnation. At length the
fulness of time came, the prophecies were fulfilled,
and the Only Begotten was seen in His glory,
"the Word was made flesh and dwelt amongst
us."

He came and He went, but the life and death of
Jesus Christ, God and Man, are the turning-point
in the world's history, and in that of every individual soul. He alone merited for us the sanctifying
grace by which we die to sin and live to God ;
His humanity, His sacred flesh and blood, were
the instrumental cause by which that grace was
won ; and Christ Himself is both the model of our
predestination, and its term. "All things are yours,"
says the Apostle, "for you are Christ's, and Christ
is God's " (I Cor. iii. 23).

All then depends on our nearness to Emmanuel,
on our having "God with us," and on His presence
in our midst. Now if with the Ascension that
Presence had been finally and completely withdrawn,
we should be more destitute of any visible means
of communication with God, of any outward centre

and object for our worship and love, than the Israelites were of old ; for they possessed the external signs of His spiritual presence, the Temple and the Mercy-seat, where He was sought and found. But God's gifts are without repentance, and revelation does not reverse its course. On the contrary, the Prophets had said that "the glory of the second House was to be greater than that of the former "; and Christ assured His disciples that He "would not leave them orphans," but "would be with them even to the end of the world."

Now the means appointed by His Infinite Wisdom to perpetuate His presence as God and Man in our midst, is the Blessed Sacrament. In the Incarnation He veiled His divinity under His human flesh, in poverty and abjection, for our sake ; but in the Holy Eucharist He has gone still further, and under the sacramental species He concealed even His Humanity, and there, invisible, mute and helpless, He lives in spite of insults, contempt, and sacrilege, to be our companion, guide, and strength.

Thus the Blessed Sacrament, being the continued life on earth of the Incarnate God, sums up and contains all the treasures of grace and the fulness of eternal glory. It is at once God's greatest gift to man, and the means by which man in return can make an adequate oblation to God. Sacrifice has ever been the one recognised act of worship due to God alone. But all the sacrifices of earth's best gifts, and even those of Israel, could not offer to God the worship which was His due, nor satisfy for the guilt contracted by sin. Both these ends were, however, accomplished by the sacrifice of the Cross, and in the Mass, by which, under the sacramental species of bread and wine, this sacrifice is mystically repeated, Jesus Christ is offered again as the Lamb slain in propitiation for our sins, and in adoration of the supreme Majesty of the One Eternal God.

In the Mass, as on the Cross, Christ is both Priest and Victim ; the human celebrant acts in His person, and consecrates in His name. Hence throughout the world there is but one Altar, one High Priest, and one Victim ; and the prophecy is ever being accomplished : " From the rising of the sun to the going down of the same, My name is great among the Gentiles, and in every place there is sacrifice and a clean oblation, saith the Lord of Hosts " (Malach. i. 11).

Hence we need not be surprised at the importance attached by Christians to the Sacrifice of the Mass. The disciples at Emmaus knew Our Lord in the " breaking of bread," and that great and solemn rite has been ever the central action of the Church's worship. It was the "secret" to which for centuries, only after long instruction, the baptized were initiated, as the crown and treasure of their faith ; and just as the first Christians assembled in " the upper room," or descended into the Catacombs, at peril of their lives, to assist at the sacred mysteries, so in our own country after the Reformation, when offering the holy sacrifice or assistance thereat, was punished by death, priests and laity, men and women, gladly gave their all—lands, liberty, life—for the sake of one Mass.

The Holy Eucharist is the heart of the Church's life and the source of her perfection. Her priests are detached and celibate, that, like Melchisedech, without father, without mother, without genealogy, they may offer the bread and wine. Her religious orders are begotten and her standard of holiness maintained by that food which is " the corn of the elect, and the wine springing forth virgins " (Zach. ix. 17). Mass again is the centre of her visible worship, not only because the faithful with the priest offer this common sacrifice, but even when there is no congregation present, the priest still celebrates as the public minister of the whole Church in her name and for her benefit. Hence at every Mass there is a real spiritual communion of all the faithful on earth.

Lastly, the Church invisible participates with the Church on earth in the fruits of the ineffable gift. For every Mass is offered up by Jesus

Christ, our Head, for His whole body, triumphant, militant, and suffering, in their three different states.    In union therefore with Him, it is offered for the Blessed in Heaven, in thanksgiving for their eternal bliss ; for the Church on earth, in adoration, satisfaction, thanksgiving, and petition ; and for the souls in Purgatory, to obtain relief from their sufferings and a speedy admittance to the Vision of God.

From what has been said, it is plain that Mass can be offered to God alone, and therefore the term, Mass of the Blessed Virgin or of any Saint, does not signify that Mass is offered to them, but to God in their honour ; that is, in thanksgiving for the graces bestowed upon them in this life, and for the glory they now enjoy in His Kingdom (Hay's " Sincere Christian ").

## THE CHURCH'S USE OF THE LATIN TONGUE.

A few words may be added about the Church's use of the Latin language in the Mass and in her Liturgical offices.

1. " The Apostles, according to ecclesiastical historians," Benedict XIV. (De Missa) writes, " not only preached but celebrated the Divine Offices in the vulgar tongue of the people in whose

land they preached the Gospel." Hence St. Peter finding throughout the West the Latin tongue prevalent, composed in that language the Liturgy of the Roman Church. When in time the Latin tongue fell into disuse, the Church still retained the original Liturgy as written by St. Peter out of respect to its founder. In this matter the new Dispensation followed the example of the old. The Jewish Scriptures were written in the Hebrew language as spoken by the Jews at the time of their production. Subsequently that tongue underwent many variations, but the language of the Scriptures was never changed. Even after the Captivity, when Syro-Chaldaic became the vernacular of the Jews, Hebrew was still the language both of the Temple and the Synagogue. Our Lord formally approved the practice by following it Himself (Luke iv. 17), and His last prayer on the Cross, " Eli, Eli, lama sabacthani " (Matt. xxvii. 47), was in the Hebrew tongue.

2. The invariable employment of the language first used has guarded the Liturgy from dangerous innovations, which would necessarily have arisen had the vernacular been introduced with its ever-changing idioms.

. 3. Uniformity of public worship is thus securely preserved. A Catholic hears one and the same tongue in whatever part of the globe he enters a

church.    Out of the 949 Archiepiscopal and Epis-
copal Sees in communion with Rome, only 77
belong to the Oriental Rite.    The Latin Rite is
therefore practically universal.

4. As the Mass is one common sacrifice of priest
and people, and is offered up by the priest in their
name and on their behalf, it is not necessary that they
should follow every word he says.   On the contrary,
the Rubric enjoins that the most solemn part, the
Canon, should be inaudible to all but the celebrant,
the whole action being between the priest and God.
In the Oriental Rite, during the Canon, the priest is
not only unheard but is also unseen, being hidden
by curtains drawn across the sanctuary doors.

5. As a fact, the faithful do understand the
Church's Latin from the action or rite accompanying
the words.    The poorest of her children in a
Catholic land know by heart, without book or
learning, large portions of her Offices, and many of
her Psalms, Hymns, and Litanies ; and the fervour
with which they join in the prayers and singing,
shows unmistakably their appreciation of the sense
and beauty of the Church's Liturgy.    Many persons
who have had long experience of the Anglican
vernacular services have testified that they first
realised the true meaning of Psalm and Prophecy
when set before them in the Liturgical language of
the Church, interpreted by her rites and ceremonies.

To face p. 45.

ST. PETER'S STATUE.

## CHAPEL OF ST. WILFRID.

Beyond the statue of St. Peter, on the north side of the eastern transept, we pass through two fine columns of verd-antique into the Chapel of St. Wilfrid. This spacious chapel, measuring about 45 by 25 feet, is surmounted by a cupola and terminates in an apse containing the Altar. At the southern end facing the apse is a small organ gallery. The columns and pilasters of this chapel are of Devonshire marble, with Carrara capitals and bases resting on pedestals of red serpentine. The Altar formed originally the central portion of the High Altar of the " Groote Kerke " of St. Servatius, the ancient cathedral of Maestricht. It is composed of various marbles of the Low Countries, and was constructed about 1710, being in the style of that period. Above the altar, on a throne enclosed by clustered marble columns, stands a statue of St. Wilfrid (at present in terra-cotta), by Mr. Codina Langlin. The chapel was decorated by Mr. J. Cosgreave.

The walls of the chapel are now faced with Mexican onyx, a rare and beautiful marble of very delicate colouring and almost pellucid transparency. A series of pictures of English saints, on rough tapestry canvas, occupy the panels. Beginning with the left-hand panel on entering, the subjects

are : St. Winefride, Virgin and Martyr ; St. Gregory
Blessing St. Augustine and his Companions on their
Mission to England ; The Death of St. Bede on com-
pleting his translation of the Gospels ; St. Edward
Giving Alms to St. John the Apostle under the garb
of a Beggar ; The Martyrdom of St. Thomas à
Becket ; St. Alban, the Protomartyr of England.

## ST. WILFRID.

The great St. Wilfrid, whose glory it was to
secure the happy links which bound England to
Rome, was born about the year 634, and was
trained by the Celtic monks at Lindisfarne in the
peculiar rites and usages of the British Church.
Yet even as a boy Wilfrid longed for perfect
conformity in discipline, as in doctrine, with the
Holy See, and at the first chance set off himself for
Rome.    On his return, he founded at Ripon a
strictly Roman monastery, under the rule of St.
Benedict, and at the Council of Whitby obtained
the adoption of the Roman Easter.    In 664 he was
elected Bishop of Lindisfarne, and five years later
was transferred to the See of York.    He had to
combat the passions of wicked kings, the cowardice
of worldly prelates, the errors of holy men.    He
was twice exiled and once imprisoned ; yet the
battle which he fought was won.    He swept away

*From Phophyle by Valentine & Sons.*

*To face p. 46.*

CHAPEL OF ST. WILFRID.

the abuses of many years and a too national system, and substituted instead a vigorous Catholic discipline, modelled and dependent on Rome. Sternly uncompromising in matters of principle, Wilfrid was a most tender Father with his flock. During his exile he converted the Friesland savages by his kindly ways, and taught the men of Sussex to fish while he won their souls to God. He died October 12, A.D. 709, and at his death was heard the sweet melody of the angels conducting his soul to Christ.

The name of St. Wilfrid is closely connected with the London Oratory through its co-founder and first Superior, Fr. Wilfrid Faber. A Yorkshireman by birth, he was baptized at the parish Church of St. Wilfrid's, Calverley, in the West Riding; he was ordained a Protestant Deacon in St. Wilfrid's old Cathedral at Ripon, and the Church spire that overlooked the garden at his living of Elton, was that of Undalum of Oundle, where St. Wilfrid died.

As an Anglican clergyman, his life of the Saint (Oxford, "Lives of English Saints," 1842, Toovey, 1845), provoked much hostile comment by its unmistakably Catholic tone. St. Wilfrid's unswerving opposition to anything like nationalism in religion, and his devotion to Roman usages and discipline, were singled out for a glowing eulogy. "He, Wilfrid," we read, "saw that the one thing to do was to go to Rome, and to learn under the shadow of St. Peter's Chair the more perfect way. To look Romeward is a Catholic instinct seemingly implanted in us for the safety of the faith " (p. 4). Loyalty to the Holy See is in fact the key-note of the biography, and when Fr. Faber's conversion followed in 1845, he took St. Wilfrid as his patron, and was confirmed in his name. He dedicated to the Saint his first Catholic Church at Cotton Hall, Derbyshire, and chose St. Wilfrid's Day for the formal foundation of the London Oratory, on which Feast the triennial elections of the Officers of the Community are still held.

From another point of view St. Wilfrid's character was especially sympathetic to Fr. Faber as an Oratorian. The Saxon Saint is described as "a quick walker, expert at all good works, and with never a sour face " : and of St. Philip we read that " no one ever saw him sad." Both taught their disciples to serve the Lord with gladness of heart ; both showed by their lives that coldness, stiffness, and gloom are no mark of true religion ; and that joy is the Christian's inheritance, the pledge of his adoption, and the secret of his strength to persevere.

## ST. CECILIA.

The left-hand bay of St. Wilfrid's Chapel contains, in a shrine of rare marbles, an exact reproduction

*To face p. 48.*

SHRINE OF ST. CECILIA.

of Stefano Maderno's figure of the Virgin and Martyr, St. Cecilia, the original of which is in the Church dedicated to that Saint in the Trastevere, Rome. "On the evening of her wedding-day, with the music of the marriage hymn ringing in her ears, Cecilia, a rich and noble Roman maiden, renewed the vow by which she had consecrated her virginity to God. 'Pure be my heart and undefiled my flesh ; for I have a Lover you know not of, an Angel of my Lord.' The heart of her young husband, Valerian, was moved by her words ; he received baptism, and within a few days he and his brother, Tiburtius, also sealed their confession with their blood. At length Cecilia's conflict came, and the Prefect, Almachius, enraged at her boldness in professing the Christian religion, commanded her to be led to her own house, there to be suffocated in a bath heated seven times its wont. But as with the Three Children, so was it with her. 'The flames had no power over her body, neither was a hair of her head singed.' The lictor sent to despatch her, struck with trembling hand the three blows which the law allowed, and left her still alive. For two days and nights Cecilia lay with her head half-severed, on the pavement of her bath, fully sensible and joyfully awaiting her crown." On the third morning, when the holy Bishop Urban visited the dying martyr—"I have prayed," she

said, " not to die till I could recommend to your care
the poor whom I have always nourished, and could
make over to you this house, that it may be a
Church for ever."    Then, turning her face towards
the ground, and folding her hands like one in sleep,
she passed to the presence of God, A.D. 177.

Her holy relics were deposited in the Catacombs,
and were lost sight of till their discovery in A.D. 821,
by Pope St. Paschal I. ; when they were translated
with honour from the Catacombs to the stately
Church which had risen on the site of the old house
of the Saint across the Tiber.    Eight centuries
later, the tomb was again opened at the desire of
Cardinal Sfondrato, who as a youth had become
intimate with St. Philip, and had imbibed from him
a fervent devotion to the early martyrs.    The body
was found incorrupt, exactly as Paschal had left
it, with the stains of blood still visible on the
Saint's gold-embroidered robe, and on the linen
used to stanch her wounds.    For a month the
sacred relics remained exposed to the sight and
veneration of the faithful ; and on November 22,
1599, Pope Clement VIII., in the presence of the
entire College of Cardinals, solemnly celebrated
Mass, and deposited the cypress coffin in a silver
casket, and replaced once more the marble slab
over the tomb.    But before this was done, Stefano
Maderno, the most celebrated sculptor then in

Rome, took a sketch of the holy body as it lay, and reproduced it afterwards in white marble. The memory of this holy Virgin and Martyr has ever been dear to the children of the Church. Painters in all ages have offered her the homage of their art. The picture over her shrine in this chapel is a careful copy of one of Raphael's masterpieces in the Gallery of Bologna. Emblems of profane music are scattered at her feet. Her hands scarce hold the instrument, from which the pipes are falling ; her eyes are raised to Heaven as she listens to Angelic Choirs. Music claims the Roman Virgin as its special Patroness. She is the Queen of Christian harmony ; even at the present day, the Feast of St. Cecilia is celebrated wherever music creates the slightest interest. Here, in London, annually on her Feast (November 22) an Oratorio is given in the Chapel of the Brothers of the Little Oratory, of whom she is fitly chosen Patroness.

Our own English poet, Pope, in his ode written to celebrate St. Cecilia's day, has said, speaking of music :

*Of Orpheus now no more let poets tell,*
*To bright Cecilia greater power is given;*
*His numbers raised a shade from Hell,*
*Hers lift the soul to Heaven.*

## OUR LADY OF GOOD COUNSEL.

Facing St. Cecilia, in a rich frame of gilded clouds and supported by cherubs, is a copy of the picture of our Lady of Good Counsel in her famous shrine at Genazzano, near Rome.

" The pious tradition," to use the words of Benedict XIV. as to the origin of this devotion, is as follows. In the fifteenth century, the ancient Church of our Lady of Good Counsel at Genazzano was being rebuilt at the cost of a devout and aged widow named Petruccia. Though she had given her all, her means proved unequal to the task, and her undertaking being brought to a standstill, Petruccia and her unfinished walls were an object of universal ridicule. Still her courage did not fail ; she had begun the work for the honour of the Mother of God, and had no fear but that our Lady would carry it through. On April 25, 1457, the Feast of our Lady of Good Counsel, while multitudes were gazing at the roofless shrine, strains of celestial harmony were heard, the bells pealed spontaneously, a white cloud was seen to settle on the roofless wall of Petruccia's Church, and within was disclosed the picture of our Lady of Good Counsel and her Divine Son. Shouts of "Evviva Maria" broke forth, and Petruccia's triumph was complete. The

*From Phophyle by Valentine & Sons.*     *To face p. 52.*

ALTAR OF OUR LADY OF GOOD COUNSEL

picture was styled "Madonna del Paradiso," in the
belief that it had been painted by the angels who
had brought it to its present site.   Yet another
marvel followed : there arrived two pilgrims, who
declared that this identical picture was from a shrine
of our Lady at Scutari in Albania, where, owing
to the spread of Mahomedanism, faith and purity
were alike decaying ; that it had been transported
across the waters of the Adriatic, how they knew
not, and that they too, in some mysterious manner,
had been borne in its wake.   At Rome it had
disappeared, and they had only found it now by
being attracted to Genazzano through rumours of
the miracle which had taken place.

Such is the tradition ; and for four centuries
since the events above narrated are said to have
occurred, the sanctuary of Genazzano has been a
source of grace and blessing to innumerable pilgrims, from every part of the world.   The humble
shrine is a Bethel where the soul finds its God, a
Bethsaida where the lame and impotent have been
healed by the Giver of life.

The brief "injunctæ brevis" of Benedict XIV.,
July 2, 1753, grants to all who join the Pious
Union, a branch of which is established at the
Oratory, on the performance of certain conditions,
the same favours as are obtained by a visit to the
shrine itself.

## THE LADY ALTAR.

We now retrace our steps to the eastern Transsept, and find ourselves in front of the Lady Altar. Two panels on each side of the Altar table bear the following inscriptions :

<table>
<tr><td>D. O. M.</td><td>D. O. M.</td></tr>
<tr><td>VIRGINI ROSARIÆ</td><td>FRANUS PATER</td></tr>
<tr><td>ARAM POSUIT</td><td>DOMUS ET ANTUS</td></tr>
<tr><td>CONFRATERNITAS</td><td>EIUS FILII</td></tr>
<tr><td>ANNO</td><td>DI CORBARELLIS</td></tr>
<tr><td>M.D.C.XCIII.</td><td>FLORENT. ARCH.</td></tr>
</table>

*"This altar was erected by the Confraternity to the Great and Good God, and to the Virgin of the Rosary in the year 1693. It was constructed by Francis di Corbarellis, and his sons Dominic and Antony."*

This Altar originally belonged to the Dominican Church in Brescia, North Italy, which was rebuilt in the seventeenth century, when the chapel of the Rosary was added ; and the Altar was erected from the design, it is believed, of Sandrino, a celebrated perspective painter of that period, who designed and executed the decoration of the whole Church. Francis di Corbarellis and his sons, Antony and Dominic, executed the marble work, as the left panel tells us.

The Church remained in the peaceable possess-

To face p. 54

THE LADY ALTAR.

sion of the Dominicans, the lawful owners, till
1797, when a revolution, instigated by the French,
drove out the Venetian Republic, then masters
of the Duchy of Brescia. The new Provisional
Government suppressed the Dominicans, seized their
property, turned the convent into a hospital, and
placed the Church under the charge of a secular
priest. By the Concordat of 1804, Pius VII. healed
or condoned the acts of the Government of 1797
regarding ecclesiastical property, and the State
thereby obtained a title to the possession of the
Church and its contents. In 1859, the Church was
converted into a hospital for the wounded after the
battle of Solferino, and the Chapel of the Rosary
was finally closed, and in 1885, both church and
chapel, having been previously stripped, were
levelled to make room for some public baths.

But, it may be asked, how was such a valuable
work of art as the Altar-piece, allowed to leave
Italy? In reply it must be remembered that in
1886, the " Liberal" Government of that country
carried out their threatened confiscation of the
property of the religious Orders, and that the same
penal law forbad the foundation of any new houses.
Hence the contents of their churches glutted the
market, and the Lady Altar, originally valued at
£16,000, was purchased, repaired, and erected for
a comparatively small sum, by the energy and self-

sacrifice of the late Fr. Keogh, of the London Oratory. The whole composition is 21 feet wide and 45 feet high, and therefore exactly fits, by a strange coincidence, its present site.   Fifteen noble figures in Carrara marble enrich its base, sides, and pediments.   Each of the larger ones would cost, according to the prices of any eminent modern sculptor, from £800 to £1000. The Saints all belong to the Dominican Order.   On either side of the base are St. Pius V., St. Philip's contemporary and friend, and St. Rose of Lima, the flower of the New World, the first canonised Saint of South America.   In the lateral niches are St. Dominic, the Patriarch and Founder of the Order, distinguished by the hound and flaming torch (Domini canis) symbolical of the sacred science, with which the sons of St. Dominic and, above all, the great St. Thomas, the prince of theologians, were to enlighten the world.   Facing St. Dominic is St. Catherine of Siena, the Seraphic Virgin.   On the superstructure are allegorical figures of Faith and Charity ; on the central arch repose the Prophets Elias and Jeremias ; while three Cherubs crown the pediment.   Two winged angels, originally on either side of the altar, are now in the organ gallery, facing St. Mary Magdalene's Chapel. "The marbles of which the altar is composed," says *The Tablet*, April 5, 1884, " are the finest that Italy could produce, and are inlaid with designs of the most beautiful description, containing, in all the central and prominent panels, roses and lilies (both allusive to the Blessed Virgin); and, in the remainder, birds, insects, fruit, flowers, vases, and an endless variety of floral scrolls; here lapis lazuli, there rock crystal, agate, and mother-of-pearl, amethysts, and red cornelian—figures standing, figures recumbent, angels on the wing, and other groups emblematical, in statuary marble; all appropriately distributed to make up one of the grandest compositions that the world ever witnessed. Here it stands after an existence of two hundred years in its native land, restored and slightly remodelled to suit its new home, a ray of light from the period of the Renaissance, to be reflected to posterity through the rescuing hand of the London Oratory."

And when all this is said, it must be remembered that we are only looking at one-half the treasures of the original chapel. The walls were likewise of Languedoc, enriched with panels of inlaid precious marbles, displaying monograms of our Lady, festoons of roses and lilies, and other appropriate devices; and thus reflected the splendour of the Altar-piece.

Now, alas! the altar stands desolate in the midst of a plaster expanse. As a portion of the original walls line the hall, staircase, and dining-room of Surrey House, Hyde Park Place, London, is it too

much to hope that they may be reproduced here, or
that, at least, some more fitting frame for the Lady
Altar may be found?    The silver Spanish lamp in
front of the Lady Altar is in memory of Ellen
Michaela Luling, 1893.

## DEVOTION TO THE BLESSED VIRGIN.

It may be well to explain here briefly the honour
paid to the Saints and Angels, and, above all, to
the Blessed Virgin, and to the images which represent them.    By the first commandment we are
commanded to pay to God supreme, divine
worship, which is due to him alone as our one
Sovereign Creator.    But besides this supreme worship, we are bound implicitly by the same commandment to honour and reverence proportionately
all who are His.    And in this respect all creatures
claim our honour, but especially those who are near
Him, or represent His authority or any special
attributes of His.    Thus we are told to " Honour
our Father and Mother," to " Fear God and honour
the King": that is, we are to pay them a real
though inferior honour.    Now it is precisely this
inferior honour, different not only in degree but
also in kind from the homage due to the Creator,
that the Church pays to the Angels and Saints;
and the practice of praising God in them (Psalm cl.),
and of blessing His holy Mother (Luke i. 48),

*To face p. 58.*

· MADONNA AND ANGELS.

VESTIBULE SACRISTY THE ORATORY.

far from derogating from the supreme homage due to Him, is part of that very worship. On the same principle, the honour paid to the Blessed Virgin stands alone : her Office and her holiness place her in a rank apart. The fact that the Son of God took flesh of her flesh and bone of her bone, the authority she exercised over Him during the long years He willed to be subject to her (Luke ii. 51), the fulness of her grace (Luke i. 30), and her own immaculate purity, all these claim a homage essentially different indeed, and infinitely below that which we pay to God, yet immensely above what we owe to any other creature. Hence her altars multiply, and her image is found in every Catholic land ; and in aspiration and prayer the name of the Mother is linked spontaneously with that of her Son. In our own land, once our Lady's dowry, 430 Catholic churches under various titles, are dedicated to the Mother of God.

## PRAYERS TO THE SAINTS.

But, it is said, does all this warrant our praying either to her or the saints ? Is there not but "one Mediator of God and man, the man Christ Jesus" (1 Tim. ii. 5) ? First, then, the prayers to the saints essentially differ from those offered to God. We ask God to *hear* us, the saints to *pray*

for us, and the intercessory prayers of angels and
saints and of the Blessed Virgin are alike offered
only through the mediation of Jesus Christ; for
creatures are heard only through Him, He alone is
heard of His own right.    As to the authority for
this practice, God might have, had He willed it,
made us pray exclusively and directly to Himself;
but He has willed to display His mercy and power
by giving efficacy to the intercessions of the just.
By their prayers Moses obtained mercy for Israel
(Exodus xxxii. 11, 14); Samuel defeated the Philis-
tines (1 Samuel vii. 8, 9, 10); only through the
prayers of Job did his friends find the grace they
were unable to obtain by themselves.    So also in
the new Law.    In the Lord's Prayer we are taught
to offer prayers for others, and to depend in turn
on theirs, and thus we learn both charity and
humility.    Christ again commanded us to pray
even for our enemies (Matt. v. 44); and St. Paul
repeatedly begged the prayers of his disciples for
himself (Eph. vi. 18, 19; 1 Tim. ii. 1).    If then
it be right and proper to ask the prayers of our
brethren here on earth, because of our fellow-
membership in Christ, still more ought we to have
recourse to those who are united with us through
the perfect charity of Heaven.    This is the meaning
of the Communion of Saints; the poorest child,
the nameless, homeless outcast, can claim through

his Christian birthright this fellowship (Eph. ii. 19),
and the Jerusalem which is above as his Mother
(Galat. iv. 26). The reality of this Communion is
shown abundantly in Holy Writ. As the devil,
our adversary, is " wandering about, seeking whom
he may devour " (1 Peter v. 8), so the angels watch
over us from our infancy (Matt. xviii. 10), and
"keep us in all our ways" (Psalm xci. 11, 12).
They are keen and earnest spectators of our
Christian combat (1 Cor. iv. 9); they bring holy
aspirations ; they assist at the Divine Sacrifice ;
and our prayers ascend as incense from out the
Angel's hand (Apoc. viii. 4). If through frailty
we fall, they rejoice when we do penance (Luke xv.
10). Saints and Angels break out into triumphant
praise when our accuser is cast forth (Apoc. xii.
10). The question whether the practice of invoking
the Saints detracts from the supreme honour due to
God or not, is one which can be decided by a
practical test. Two great rites of religion are
proper to God alone : He alone can receive sacrifice ;
He alone can give sacramental grace. Where do
we find sacrifice most constantly offered and Sacraments most constantly administered ? Where are
they of grave obligation ? In the Churches where
the invocation of the Blessed Virgin and the Saints
is enjoined, or in those where it is proscribed ?

## PURGATORY.

On the right of the Lady Altar is a picture representing the Holy Souls in Purgatory, a subject which requires a few words of explanation. The very idea of retributive justice in time or eternity is now often regarded as incompatible with the notion of a good God; yet the doctrine of punishment, and even of eternal punishment, is an essential part of Christ's teaching. Christ became man that the world might not perish, but have eternal life, and He recognises no alternative but an equally endless death. It is better, He says, to go into life maimed or lame, than with two hands and feet to be cast into everlasting fire (Matt. xviii. 8). And the issue of our probation is pronounced in one of two judgments. "Depart, ye cursed, to everlasting fire"; or "Come, ye Blessed, to the Kingdom prepared for you from the foundation of the world" (Matt. xxiv. 31). And this has been the Christian belief from the first. It was no mere natural enthusiasm, nor attachment to a cause, nor even divine charity alone, but the conviction of the eternal loss inevitably consequent on apostasy, which made the first Christians—poor cobblers, or slaves, or trembling women and children—strong in their confession under torture and death.

And if we turn to a later period and take Dante as an exponent of Christian faith in the Middle Ages, his one conception of human life, its value and purpose, is that every man and woman is tending day by day to Heaven or Hell. For every child of Adam is created intellectual, free, and immortal, and fully endowed by grace for the attainment of his last end, eternal bliss in God. The dire punishments of the Inferno are therefore the necessary consequence of individual guilt of the persistent, wilful, final rejection of the divine mercy. So far from being opposed to divine good-ness is the infliction of the punishment, in Dante's mind, that he makes it the very office of divine charity thus to chastise any assailant of the eternal moral order, and so preserve it intact.

> *Justice, the founder of my fabric moved :*
> *To rear me was the task of power divine,*
> *Supremest wisdom, and primeval love.*
> HELL, III. 4.

With regard to Purgatory, the principles on which it is based and the nature of the purification itself, are both found in Holy Writ and in the primitive discipline of the Church.

First, there is the explicit statement that nothing defiled can enter Heaven, and that, without holiness, no man can see God. And since but few can arrive at such purity in this life, it follows that those lesser moral defects, "the idle word," and the remains and consequences of graver past sins, which are found at death even in the souls of the just, have to be cleansed away hereafter. In this sense are interpreted the words of Christ of the forgiveness in the world to come (Matt. xii. 32), and of the debtor who only escapes from prison after paying the uttermost farthing (Matt. v. 25). So also is St. Paul's teaching that "the fire shall try every man's works, and that many shall be saved, yet so as by fire" (1 Cor. iii. 13, 14, 15); and St. Peter's statement of Christ preaching to the spirits "who were sometime disobedient" (1 Peter iii. 18, 19, 20); which implies a middle place, as the spirits preached to could not have been in hell. Again, we know from 2 Machab. xii. 46, that it was the custom of the Jews, long before Christ's coming, to offer prayers and sacrifices for the dead; and the antiquity of the doctrine in the Church is shown by the fact that prayers for the dead are found in every ancient Liturgy, and on the earliest Christian tombs.

The consolation afforded by this practice robs death of half its worst sting. Our power to help those we love no longer ends with the grave. On the contrary, as their time of merit is past, and they cannot help themselves, they depend more than ever on us for the peace they seek. Most beautiful and touching are the brief appeals for prayers on a Catholic grave : " Martini Luigi implora pace." " Lucrezia Picini implora eterna quiete." From the Certosa at Bologna, or, again, from the Catacombs, the Intercessions in their behalf : "Vale Sabina vivas in Deo dulcis ;" " Farewell, Sabina, mayst thou live sweet in God," " In pace Domini dormias," "Mayst thou sleep in the peace of the Lord ;" or the constant Requiescat in pace, " May He rest in Peace."

The teaching of Purgatory, as a revelation at once of the justice and mercy of God, is beautifully drawn out in Cardinal Newman's poem, " The Dream of Gerontius." The separated soul darts forth with the intemperate energy of love, to unite itself to God, its only Good, but because of its remaining stains, falls scorched and shrivelled by the " fire of sanctity," which " circles round the Crucified."

> *And these two pains, so counter and so keen,*
> *The longing for Him when thou seest Him not,*
> *The shame of self at thought of seeing Him,*
> *Will be thy veriest, sharpest Purgatory.*

Yet in all its sufferings are solaced by the unutterable peace of pardon pronounced, and it is thus both

> *Consumed, yet quickened, by the glance of God.*

E

Lastly, the soul is sustained by the hope of its release, of which the Angel assures it :

> *Farewell, but not for ever, brother dear,*
> *Be brave and patient on thy bed of sorrow;*
> *Swiftly shall pass thy night of trial here,*
> *And I will come and wake thee on the morrow.*

## CALVARY.

From the Lady Chapel we now enter the Calvary, above which is the organ chamber. The Calvary, as is usual, contains three crosses, that of our Blessed Lord being in the centre, and on the right and left those of the good and bad thief. The great mystery of our Redemption is often strangely misrepresented as the compulsory and vindictive punishment of the innocent for the guilty. The Catholic doctrine, on the contrary, is that the whole merit of Christ's Passion and Death arises from the fact that, of no necessity but of His own free will, He offered himself " for us men, and for our salvation." He was both Priest and Victim, and it was His infinite love, not His physical sufferings by themselves, which gave to His Sacrifice an infinite value. Secondly, while, according to Luther and Calvin, the salvation of the Elect follows necessarily, without regard to their interior dispositions, from the external imputation of the merits of Christ, the Church teaches that the fruit of Christ's death profits only on the performance of the conditions prescribed—faith, repentance, &c. ; for personal guilt can never be cancelled without a repentant will. Finally, the Catholic Church teaches, that though God will not save us without our co-operation, yet no natural powers, by themselves, can advance us one step towards a supernatural reward. And consequently we can work out our salvation only by the aid of grace won for us by Christ's death, from the first moment of justification to the last act of charity which crowns the probation of the just.

Such is the Christian doctrine of Redemption. God might, had He willed, have pardoned us gratuitously, for sin is committed against Him alone ; or He might have accepted the imperfect satisfaction of the creature ; or Christ might have saved us by a single sigh or tear, for all His acts were of infinite value. He willed, however, to suffer and die, and to shed His last drop of Blood, to show us the greatness of His love, the malice of sin, and the value of our souls, bought by so great a price.

As to the teaching of the Crucifix, rightly understood, Cardinal Newman shall speak : " It is the very idea, that He is God, which gives a meaning

to His sufferings; what is to me a man, and
nothing more, in agony, or scourged, or crucified ?
There are many holy martyrs, and their torments
were terrible.    But here I see One dropping blood,
gashed by the thong, and stretched upon the
Cross, and He is God.    It is no tale of human
woe which I am reading here ; it is the record of
the Passion of the great Creator.    The Word and
Wisdom of the Father, who dwelt in His bosom in
bliss ineffable from all eternity, whose very smile
has shed radiance and grace over the whole crea-
tion, whose traces I see in the starry heavens and
on the green earth, this glorious living God, it is
He who looks at me so piteously, so tenderly from
the Cross.    He seems to say: I cannot move,
though I am omnipotent, for sin has bound
me here"    ("Sermons to Mixed Congregations,"
Disc. xv.).


## THE PIETÀ.

On the right of the Crucifix is a small
plaster Pietà, a term denoting the Mother of
Sorrows with her dead Son on her lap.    The
part of the Blessed Virgin in the Passion has. been
fully treated in the notice of the Seven Dolours
Chapel.    Of this special mystery Cardinal Newman

again says : "Think you not, that to Mary, when
she held Him in her maternal arms, when she

THE PIETÀ.

gazed on the pale countenance and the dislocated
limbs of her God, when she traced the wandering

lines of blood, when she counted the weals, the bruises, and the wounds, which dishonoured that virginal flesh, think you not that to her eyes it was more beautiful than when she first worshipped it, pure, radiant, and fragrant, on the night of His nativity ? " (" Sermons to Mixed Congregations," Disc. xiv.).

## ST. FRANCIS.

On the right of the Pietà is a striking picture, probably Spanish, of St. Francis, the " Poor Man of Assisi." He gave away all his earthly wealth, and one poor tunic and cord girdle showed how dear was his love of " the Lady Poverty," his now chosen spouse. She brought him, as her dowry, a marvellous sense of perpetual dependence on God, and of the obligation of constant thanksgiving for his Heavenly Father's care. Over the Umbrian Hills, he would be heard singing his " Cantico del sole," in which he " praised God for all His gifts— for the sun and its shining splendour, bringing day and light and speaking, O Lord, of Thee, for our sister, the water so pure and precious (casta e pretiosa), for our mother the earth, and her divers fruits and flowers, for all who peaceably endure injuries and weakness and tribulation ; " " for

Thou, O most Highest, shalt give them a crown."
" Praised be my Lord," he concludes, " for our sister,
the death of the body, from which no man escapeth.
Woe to him who dieth in mortal sin.    Blessed are
they who are found walking by Thy most Holy
Will, for the second death shall do them no harm.
Praise ye and bless the Lord, and give thanks unto
Him, and serve Him with great humility."

Thus did Francis realise to the letter the Beati-
tudes of the Gospel, their conditions, and their
reward.    His prayer, " May I die to the world for
the love of Thy love, who didst die on the Cross
for love of my love," was wonderfully answered.
His worn and emaciated body was stamped with
the Five Sacred Wounds, and he bore in his hands
and feet and side the stigmata of his crucified
Lord.

It is no wonder that a Saint who was thus a
living likeness of his Lord, should have evoked in
an age of faith the homage of multitudes.    His
Order numbered 5000 Friars in his own lifetime :
Cimabue and Giotto painted his likeness; St. Louis,
King of France, St. Elizabeth of Hungary, and a
long line of Prelates and Princes enrolled themselves as Tertiaries under his guidance.    This
Third Order for the laity has been especially com-
mended by the present Pope, as embodying the
true principles of Christian poverty, charity, and

humility, in opposition to the false equality, frater-
nity, and liberty taught by the Sects.


## ST. JOHN BAPTIST DE ROSSI.

Opposite the picture of St. Francis is that of
St. John Baptist de Rossi.   Like St. Philip, his
special model, he lived and died in Rome, and
attained to sanctity by the daily self-sacrificing
apostolate of a secular priest, being unremitting
in his labours in the confessional and in minister-
ing to the poor and the sick.   The Hospital of the
Trinità dei Pellegrini, the Confraternity of which
was founded by St. Philip in 1550, was the chief
scene of his labours.   In his last illness, the life
of St. Philip was his chosen book, and he died
during the Novena of St. Philip, May 23, 1764,
three days before the Saint's Feast.

This portrait of St. John Baptist de Rossi is
copied from the original likeness of the Saint at
his altar in the chapel of St. Trinità dei Pellegrini,
where his body lies.   It was presented to the
Oratory by Mr. Alderman Stuart Knill (Lord
Mayor of London, 1892–93), on behalf of the
Confraternity of the Blessed Sacrament of "The
Star of the Sea" Church, at Greenwich, which is
affiliated to that of the St. Trinità.   The Confra-

ternity of the Blessed Sacrament pays an annual visit to the Oratory, to do homage to this Saint on his Feast, May 23.

## THE ORGAN.

Over the Calvary is the Choir and Organ. The organ was constructed by Messrs. Bishop and Son, of 250 Marylebone Road, for the old Church of the Oratory in 1858. It underwent considerable enlargement and alteration on being placed in the new Church in 1884 ; the keyboard was reversed, pneumatic action applied to the great organ and couplers, and several new stops were added. There are four manuals and 61 stops, the total number of pipes being 4106. The organ is blown by a 3½-horse gas-engine, supplying five different pressures of wind, the engines and feeders being placed in a crypt about 30 feet below the instrument.

It will not, perhaps, be without interest to give some account of St. Philip's connection with sacred music, and the influence which he exercised upon it in his day. "Our Saint was profoundly convinced," says his latest biographer, Cardinal Capecelatro, "that there is in music and in song a mysterious and a mighty power to stir the heart with high and noble emotions, and an especial

fitness to raise it above sense to the love of heavenly
things ; hence it was that he gave it a foremost
place in his thoughts and plans ; and in the various
exercises of prayer in the Oratory, in the visits of
devotion to the Seven Churches, and in the recrea-
tions he invented for the Roman youths, music and
singing had·always a prominent part." As a consequence, his Oratory became one of the chief
centres of sacred music in Rome, his singers as
well as his composers being selected from the most
celebrated artists of the time. The exercises of
devotion, as there practised, offered to composers
a wider field for their art than even the great
Basilicas ; for besides the Masses, Psalms, and Anti-
phons which were all sung to figured music, there
were in use at the Oratory a great many " Laudi,"
motetts and madrigals in the vernacular, which it
was customary to sing before and after the sermons
every afternoon, and which gave scope for a more
popular style of composition. At St. Philip's desire,
many of these were set to music by Giovanni
Animuccia, one of his penitents, eminent both in
piety and in musical ability, who had been appointed
choirmaster of St. Peter's under Pope Julius III.
This distinguished musician used to go every day
to sing at the Oratory after the sermons, taking
with him many of his companions. He died in
1571, in the arms of his beloved Father Philip, and

the Saint had to look for one to succeed him in his
office. There was one to whom such a work
would indeed be a labour of love, for in addition to
the eminent place he held in his art, he had been
from his youth closely knit in friendship with
Philip and had long taken him for his spiritual
guide; this one was Giovanni Pierluigi da Palestrina.

The state of sacred music had become so debased
in the first half of the sixteenth century, that the
Council of Trent issued injunctions for a rigorous
reform. Among the Cardinals appointed to see
these injunctions carried into effect, was St.
Charles Borromeo, the intimate friend of St. Philip.
The task was a difficult one, and, perhaps at the
prompting of our Saint, it was entrusted to Palestrina. The success of his labours exceeded all
hopes, and the now famous Mass entitled " Papæ
Marcelli," which he wrote as an example of what
sacred music should be, was pronounced unapproach-
able in sublimity, simplicity, and beauty. When
Pius IV. heard it on June 19, 1565, he exclaimed :
"These are surely the harmonies of the new
Canticle which St. John heard sung in the Jerusalem that is above."

This decisive triumph of harmonised music must
have rejoiced Philip's heart—it was the style he had
cultivated with such care in his Oratory; and the

triumph was won by his own disciple and the friend of Animuccia. In 1571, Palestrina, at the full height of his fame, undertook the office of Maestro di Capella at the Oratory. At the Saint's request and under his direction, he wrote a number of motetts and psalms, besides setting to music a great many popular "canzoni" and hymns, now preserved in MS. in the library of the Vallicella— thus bringing the musical exercises of the Oratory to a state of high perfection. When, in the spring of 1594, Palestrina lay dying, Philip was constantly at his side with words of consolation. At dawn of day, on the Feast of the Purification (February 2), the dying man remembered with gratitude and joy that but a few days before he had composed and printed the Laudi of Mary, and this remembrance gave him renewed fervour and hope. Then Philip said to him, with a countenance lighted up with the love of God : "O my son, would it gladden you to go to enjoy the feast which to-day is held in heaven, in honour of the Queen of Angels and of Saints " ? A thrill of tender emotion passed through the heart of the dying man ; he paused a while and then answered : "Yes, surely, I do most eagerly desire it ; may Mary my advocate obtain for me this grace from her divine Son." "Scarcely had he uttered these words," says Baini, "when, in full possession of all his faculties, full of peace and trust in the mercy of the Lord, he gently breathed out his soul to God, and went, as I trust, through the intercession of the Blessed Virgin, and the prayers of his holy confessor Philip, where the song of divine praise flows on unceasingly." For more than a century after the death both of Palestrina and St. Philip, the excellence of the music performed at the Oratory was well maintained, as may be gathered from the fact that such masters as Anerio, Allegri, Carissimi, and Scarlatti were closely associated with it. The form of sacred music so popular in England at the present day, under the title of " Oratorio," owes its origin and name to the religious dramas first performed as part of the devotions in the Church of St. Philip's Oratory, these being but a development of the time-honoured " Laudi." That the music of the Oratory formed an attraction even to foreigners visiting Rome, we learn from John Evelyn, who in his Diary for November 8, 1644, says : " This evening I was invited to hear rare music at the Chiesa Nuova ; the black marble pillars within led us to that most precious Oratory of Philippus Nerius, their founder, they being of the Oratory of Secular Priests under no vow. . . . This fair church consists of fourteen altars and as many chapels. . . . Through this we went into the Sacrista, where the tapers being lighted, one of the Order preached ;

after him stepped up a child of eight or nine years
old, who pronounced an oration with so much
grace that I never was better pleased. . . . This
being finished, began their motettos, which, in a
lofty cupola richly painted, were sung by rare
voices accompanied by theorboes, harpsichords, and
viols, so that we were even ravished with the enter-
tainment of the evening."   Again, on the 20th :
" We concluded this evening with hearing the rare
voices and music at the Chiesa Nuova"; and on the
23rd, " we spent the evening at the Chiesa Nuova,
where was excellent music"; and on Easter Mon-
day, " we went to hear music in the Chiesa Nuova,
though there were abundance of ceremonies at the
other great churches."   .

It has always been the aim of St. Philip's sons
in London to carry out the traditions of their
Father in regard to sacred music.   While making
free use of the works of the great masters of the
eighteenth and present century, they are careful
not to forget those of the sixteenth, and for many
years it has been their custom to produce the
sublime compositions—too rarely heard—of Palestrina and his contemporaries, notably during the
solemn seasons of Advent and Lent.   It may be
added that there are not wanting at the present day
artists of recognised talent, who by their compositions and kindly interest  assist them generously

in their endeavour to maintain an excellence in sacred music in accordance with the traditions of their holy Founder.

## ST. PETER'S STATUE.

In front of the Calvary, and between the pillars of the Organ Gallery, is a seated statue of St. Peter, a reproduction, in wood gilt, of the bronze statue in the nave of St. Peter's, Rome. The original, according to most antiquarians, was cast from the metal of the statue of Jupiter Capitolinus, in the fifth century, by St. Leo the Great, in thanksgiving for the deliverance of the city from Attila and his Huns. The custom practised of reciting a Credo before this statue and kissing the projected foot, in sign of Catholic faith and allegiance to the Holy See, was introduced, it is said, by Baronius, the disciple of St. Philip.

## THE HOLY SEE.

The doctrine, implied in this act of homage, of the Primacy and Infallible teaching of the Roman Pontiff, as the Successor of St. Peter, is based on the following grounds : Faith in what God reveals, because He reveals it, being the first condition for salvation (Mark xvi. 16), God is bound to show us with clearness and certainty what that revelation

is. Now He has willed to do this, not by directly
communicating it to each individual soul, but
through the medium of human ministers, the
Apostles and their Successors through all time.
" Going therefore, teach ye all nations, baptizing
them in the name of the Father, and of the Son,
and of the Holy Ghost. Teaching them to observe
all things whatsoever I have commanded you, and
behold I am with you all days, even to the consum-
mation of the world." (Matt. xxviii. 19. 20).
All those who by faith, worship, and obedience
accept this teaching, form one Body, the Church,
of which Christ Himself is the Head. But in
order to ensure faith and discipline in a communion
which was to be world-wide and for all time,
Christ appointed one visible Head as His Vicar
or Vicegerent on earth. This was Peter, the
Prince of the Apostles, and on Peter alone, as the
Rock, Christ built His Church (Matt. xvi. 18).
In him resides the office of infallible teacher in
Faith and Morals. He may err and sin as a
private individual, but officially, as Head of the
Church, he is divinely protected from adding to or
taking from the Faith once delivered; for against
him "the gates of hell," or the powers of evil,
"will never prevail." To him also is given "the
Keys of Heaven," the supremacy of jurisdiction
over the universal Church. Pastors as well as

people depend on Peter, not he on them (Luke xxii. 32 ; John xxi. 15–18). This infallibility and supremacy of Peter is attested in the Acts of the Apostles. At his instigation and according to his ruling, the election of Matthias was performed. Peter punished Ananias and Sapphira, anathematised Simon Magus, the first heretic, was the first to visit and confirm the Churches which were subjected to persecution. He was the first to admit publicly to the Church the Gentile world in the person of Cornelius. St. Paul, the Apostle of the Gentiles and directly taught by God, did not enter on his Priestly office till after fifteen days' conference with St. Peter (Galatians i. 18), and the detailed explanation he deems necessary, of his opposition to Peter on the question of eating with the Gentile converts, though quoted in objection, is in fact a strong confirmatory proof of the weight he attached to that Apostle's authority. At the Council of Jerusalem, after there had been much disputing (Acts xv. 7), St. Peter gave sentence authoritatively, on which "the multitude held their peace," St. James, though Bishop of Jerusalem, also assenting to his decision.

And the supremacy thus established in Peter has endured through all time. Visible communion with the Roman See is the one recognised test of Church membership. It is with Rome, Irenæus

F

declares in the second century, because of its
pre-eminent principality, that all Churches must
agree.    Separated bodies may have Orders, Episco-
pacy, Sacraments, but outside the unity, says St.
Augustine, the Sacraments of Christ are "possessed
not unto salvation, but unto judgment."    And the
very titles of other communions show where alone
the centre of unity resides.    They are "Orthodox,"
or "Reformed," or "Old Catholic," or Catholic
with a national prefix; but *the* Catholic, the
universal Church, independent of race, or tongue,
or place, is recognised at once and always as the
Church of Rome; for "ubi Petrus, ibi Ecclesia"
("where Peter is, there is the Church"    St.
Ambrose, on Psalm lx).

## ST. PETER IN ROME.

The fact that St. Peter was the founder and
first Bishop of the Roman Church rests on evidence
of such a kind, that if it be rejected no event of the
first two centuries of the Christian era could be
regarded as certain.    The tradition in its favour is
uniform and unbroken for fourteen centuries; nor
is there the least trace of any other Church ever
having claimed to be the place of the Apostle's
death.    "All the ancients," says Baratier, a learned

Huguenot (1740), "and the great majority of
moderns, have undertaken to prove the succession
of the Bishops of Rome from the Apostle Peter.
So great in the matter has been the agreement of
all, that it ought to be deemed a miracle that
certain persons born in our own day have
presumed to deny so manifest a fact." The
"miracle" can only be accounted for by the wilful
blindness engendered by partisan prejudice. We
will content ourselves with citing some of the most
learned non-Catholic authorities on the subject.

Chamier says : "All the Fathers with great
unanimity have asserted that Peter went to Rome
and administered that Church." "To me," says
Vossius, "those appear to have no shame who deny
these things in contradiction to all antiquity, as if
in history we could know anything from any other
source than the writings of the ancients." "That
St. Peter was at Rome," says Whiston, translator
of Josephus, 1740, "is so clear in Christian
antiquity, that it is a shame for a Protestant to
confess that any Protestant ever denied it." "That
St. Peter was at Rome," says Bishop Pearson, "is
proved from Ignatius, Papias, Dionysius of Corinth,
Irenæus, Caius, Clement of Alexandria, Tertullian,
Origen, Cyprian, Lactantius, Eusebius, Athanasius,
Epiphanius, Julian the Apostate, Augustine,
Palladius. Therefore it is wonderful that there can

be found who deny that Peter ever was at Rome "
(" The Chair of Peter," by J. N. Murphy). To these
may be added Cave, E. Bunsen, Tregelles. We will
conclude with the following extract from Gibbon :
" On the spot where St. Peter suffered martyrdom,
a temple, which far surpasses the glories of the
capitol, has been since erected by the Christian
Pontiffs, who, deriving their claim of universal
dominion from a humble fisherman of Galilee, have
succeeded to the throne of the Cæsars, given laws
to the barbarian conquerors of Rome, and extended
their spiritual jurisdiction from the coast of the
Baltic to the shores of the Pacific Ocean "
(" Decline and Fall of the Roman Empire," ch.
xvi.).

## INDULGENCES.

A notice at the base of this statue states that an
indulgence of forty days may be gained by those
who practise this devotion.    As much misconcep-
tion exists about the doctrine of indulgences, a
brief explanation of the Church's teaching on this
subject may be of use.    An indulgence, then, is not
pardon for sin to come, for no power in earth or
Heaven can forgive sins without a true and hearty
contrition ; nor, still less, is it leave to commit sin,

such blasphemous doctrine being unknown in the
Church. An indulgence is the remission of
temporal punishment due to sin, after the sins
themselves have been already pardoned, as to their
guilt and eternal punishment, by repentance and
confession. Instances of temporal punishment
remaining due to forgiven sins are seen in Moses,
who, though pardoned for his sin, was forbidden
for that same sin to enter the promised land : and
in David, whose sin, though forgiven, was punished
by the death of his child. It is true that all sin,
and the whole debt of punishment due for sin,
whether in time or eternity, is forgiven only
through the death of Christ, but He has willed that
this forgiveness should be applied to our souls
through the Sacraments of Baptism and Penance.
The necessity of both Sacraments is fully shown
by the words of Holy Scripture. Of Baptism
our Lord said : " Except a man be born of water
and the Holy Ghost, he cannot enter into the
Kingdom of Heaven " (John iii. 5) ; and of Penance :
" Receive ye the Holy Ghost, whose sins you shall
forgive, they are forgiven them ; and whose sins you
shall retain, they are retained " (John xx. 23).
" This wonderful power " (Catholic Dictionary)
" must have been intended not only for the Apostles,
but for their successors likewise ; for it could
never have been Christ's purpose to limit the

means of pardon to the lifetime of his own
disciples.  As long as sin lasts, the streams of
grace and mercy must also flow."   Now Baptism
cancels not only the sin, but the whole punishment
due for it, and procures for all adults as well as
infants who die immediately after its reception,
an entrance to Heaven.   The effects of penance
are not so complete.   The Church has power to
bind and to loose (Matt. xvii. 18) sins committed
after Baptism, but because of their more perverse
malice, their temporal punishment is not remitted
by the priest's absolution, but some penance or
penitential work is appointed in satisfaction thereof.
Owing to the present mild discipline of the Church,
penance usually leaves a debt of temporal punishment still to be undergone, and it is to clear this
that indulgences are granted.   " Of course no
indulgence can free the penitent from the obliga-
tions he has incurred by the fact of repentance,
such as restoring stolen goods, retracting calumnies,
avoiding dangerous occasions ; nor from the natural
consequences of his sin, shame, sickness, and the
like " ; but it does remit the temporal punishment
which the justice of God would have further
required.   An indulgence has this power because
the Church applies to the work, performed in
obedience to her authority, the infinite satisfaction
of Christ, and the superabundant satisfaction

of the Saints. This power of inflicting and remitting penance has been exercised by the Church from the first. Thus St. Paul, in the name and in the "power of our Lord Jesus," imposed a heavy penance on the incestuous Corinthian (1 Cor. v. 4); and afterwards, because of his manifest contrition, remits it "in the person of Christ" (2 Cor. ii. 10).

In the early Church, heavy penances of many years or a lifetime were imposed for certain grave sins, but these were often curtailed, not only when the penitent gave extraordinary signs of contrition, but also when those Christians who had undergone imprisonment or torture for their faith interceded on behalf of the penitents. In process of time the penitential discipline was further modified by the substitution of shorter and milder penances for those of days, weeks, or years, imposed by the Canons. Hence comes the expression, still in use, of so many days or years' indulgence, and therefore the forty days' indulgence on the notice before us implies that the prayer carrying this privilege is equivalent, if accompanied with the necessary dispositions, to forty days of the old canonical penance. To gain an indulgence, it is not sufficient to perform the good work enjoined, but it is further required that the person performing it should be in a state of grace; for an indulgence, being a remission of the temporal *punishment* due to sin, presupposes the soul free from its guilt. The desire to gain indulgences, far from being an inducement to sin, is a powerful incentive to penance, and as they profit only in proportion to the perfect detestation of sin accompanying their performance, indulgences aid much to promote strictness of life. Lastly, the duration of the commuted canonical penance, specified in the terms of the indulgence, recalls the severity of divine justice ; while the indulgence itself is a reminder of the infinite mercy of God, and His eagerness to welcome the penitent sinner ("Cath. Dict.," art. "Indulgence ").

## ST. TERESA.

On the right, on leaving the Calvary, is a picture
of St. Teresa (d. 1582), the founder of the Reformed Carmelite Nuns, and, with St. Peter of
Alcantara and St. John of the Cross, of the Reformed Carmelite Friars. Her spiritual writings
have placed her in a rank with the first mystical
theologians. In art she is generally represented
with a Seraph wounding her heart with the dart of
divine love. The first Chapter of the Carmelite
Order in Europe was held at Aylesford in Kent,
1245, when St. Simon Stock—so called from having
lived as a hermit in the trunk or stock of a tree—
was elected Prior-General. On July 16, 1251, as
he knelt in the Whitefriars Convent at Cambridge,
praying in great distress, on account of troubles in
his Order, our Lady appeared and presented him with
the Scapular in assurance of her protection. The
devotion to the blessed habit spread quickly far
and wide, and is still most dear to the faithful.
The prayer of enrolment shows its purpose. As the
only begotten Son of God clad Himself in the

vestment of our mortality, so the habit is to be worn as a pledge of innocence and humility, and of the " putting on of Jesus Christ." Those who are affiliated to the Order by the devout use of the Scapular are under the special protection of the Blessed Virgin, and have part "in all the prayers, disciplines, fasts, alms-deeds, watching masses, divine offices, and other spiritual goods which are performed, night and day, by the Religious of the Order, through the merits of Jesus Christ." The Scapulars are given at the Lady Altar in the Oratory, after Vespers on the first Sunday of each month.

There were fifty-two houses of Carmelite Friars before the Reformation. There are now two houses of Friars and six of Carmelite Nuns.

## CHAPEL OF ST. MARY MAGDALENE.

We now enter St. Mary Magdalene's Chapel. The vault, cupola, and frieze are richly decorated with arabesques on a gold and blue ground. The doorways are of Sicilian marble, and bear in black letters "Contritio," "Dilectio" ("Sorrow," "Love") The decorations are by Mr. J. Cosgreave. The Altar, designed by Mr. H. Gribble, is of Devonshire marble with columns of Derbyshire alabaster. The

From Photphyle by Valentine & Sons.

To face p. 90.

ALTAR OF ST. MARY MAGDALENE.

central picture, by Mr. Codina Langlin, represents
the Magdalen as a youthful penitent, illuminated
with the ray from Heaven. Below the altar-table
is a sarcophagus containing the relics of St.
Eutropius, brought here from the Catacombs. The
floor is of Languedoc, Paonazzo, and Siena marble.
On either side of the altar are Venetian mosaics
representing the Magdalen washing our Lord's
feet, and His appearance to her in the garden after
the Resurrection. A Latin inscription states that
they are memorial tablets to Commander Blake,
U.S.N. In the northern niche is a very beautiful
picture of our Lord carrying His Cross, by Cima
di Conegliano (1489–1517).

## ST. MARY MAGDALENE.

" After the Blessed Virgin, no woman has been so
glorified as Mary Magdalene, of whose early life the
only record is, that ' she was a woman who was a
sinner.' From the depth of her degradation she raised
her eyes to Jesus with sorrow, hope, and love. All
covered with shame, she came to where Jesus was
at meat, and knelt behind Him. She said not a word,
but bathed His feet with her tears, wiped them with
the hair of her head, kissed them in humility, and
at their touch her sins and her stain were gone.
Then she poured on them the costly unguent

prepared for far other uses; and His own divine
lips rolled away her reproach, spoke her absolution,
and bade her go in peace. Thenceforward she
ministered to Jesus, sat at His feet, and heard His
words. She was one of the family 'whom Jesus
so loved,' that he raised her brother Lazarus from
the dead. Once again, on the eve of His Passion,
she brought the precious ointment, and, now
purified and beloved, poured it on His head, and
the whole house of God is still filled with the
fragrance of her anointing. She stood with our
Lady and St. John at the foot of the Cross, the
representative of the many who have been much
forgiven. To her first, after His Blessed Mother,
and through her to His Apostles, our Lord gave
the certainty of his Resurrection, and to her first
He made Himself known, calling her by her name
because she was His."

## THE CONFESSIONAL.

In this chapel is the Confessional chosen by our
artist for illustration. It is modelled after the type
of those found in Antwerp, where much excellent
Renaissance work was executed during the Spanish
occupation of the Low Countries. The keys and the
sponge with slate in the Angels' hands signify the
power of the Sacrament of penance to absolve and

To face p. 92.

CONFESSIONAL, ST. MARY MAGDALENE CHAPEL.

blot out sin. According to the Roman Ritual, the Confessional must be in an open, conspicuous part of the Church, and there must be a grating between the priest and the penitent.

Of the institution of this Sacrament by Christ, enough has been said under the head of Indulgences. Here it may be well to add that Absolution is not a prayer that God will pardon the sinner, nor a declaration of His merciful intent to do so, but a judicial act, by which the Priest, as judge, through Christ's authority, pardons then and there the sinner before him.

It is an article of Faith, defined by the Council of Trent (sess. xiv. can. 9), that jurisdiction is essentially necessary for validity of absolution. Jurisdiction is the power to rule—*i.e.*, to treat others as subjects, to act as judge over them ; and a priest without this power conferred on him by lawful authority can no more absolve a penitent than a magistrate could try a thief in a county where he had no commission from the Crown to do so. It is true that none but ordained priests can receive this power, nevertheless ordination, *per se*, does not confer the power to absolve. This power of jurisdiction can only be given, ordinarily speaking, by the Bishop of the Diocese in which the confession is heard, and before it is conferred proofs are required that the priest who applies for it possesses the requisite knowledge of moral theology. Jurisdiction, as a rule, is only given from year to year. A priest who hears confessions without jurisdiction, commits a grave sin of sacrilege and frustrates the Sacrament. On the part of the penitent, the confession must be entire—*i.e.*, as regards the number and kind of mortal sins, as far as possible, and accompanied with supernatural sorrow and a firm purpose of amendment; which last condition signifies a resolve to avoid not only the sin itself, but also its occasion.

## CHAPEL OF ST. PATRICK.

From St. Mary Magdalene we pass to the Chapel of St. Patrick, rich in marbles, gold and colour. The altar itself is from Naples, of the kind often found in Southern Italy. The superstructure is from the design of Mr. Gribble. The marbles are Sicilian, Fleur de Pêche, and Siena. The floor and dado and altar-rails are also of various foreign marbles. The altar picture is of St. Patrick; in the lateral niches are St. Columba and St. Bridget, all by Pietro Pezzati, a well-known Florentine artist.

The altar was erected for the Confraternity of St. Patrick, founded by Fr. Faber in 1856, to secure regular attendance at Sunday Mass, and to

*To face p. 94*

ALTAR OF ST. PATRICK.

promote devotion to the Blessed Sacrament.    The
pictures in the adjacent marble panels therefore
represent the mystery of the Holy Eucharist.
They are the manna and the multiplication of the
loaves ; above is the Last Supper.    They are also

DOORHEAD, ST. PATRICK'S CHAPEL.

by Pietro Pezzati, and are executed on canvas in
tempera or distemper, an earlier method of fresco
work, now coming back to use.    The small picture
of the Assumption on the Tabernacle door was
painted on copper by a Spanish priest, 1715.

The walls of the chapel are of Connemara and

Lessoughter marble ; the cornice is gilt, the frieze is enriched with gold arabesques.   The walls above the cornice and the diagonal panels of the vault are decorated with angels bearing scrolls and emblems allusive to the Legend of St. Patrick, the arms of the Four Provinces of Ireland, and those of Leo XIII. and of the late Cardinal Manning. The decorations of the Chapel were by Mr. Cosgreave, the panellings by Mr. Codina Langlin.

Mass, and Communion of the men and of the women of the Confraternity, are held in the chapel on the first and second Sunday of each month.

## ST. PATRICK.

" Towards the close of the fourth century, Patrick, a young Christian of Roman parentage, was tending sheep as a captive amidst the mountains of Antrim and Down.   His time was wholly given to penance and prayer.   The Psalms of David and the most beautiful hymns of the Church formed his daily petitions ; while the gift of miracles marked his favour with God.   At the age of twenty-two he was set free, and warned by a voice from Heaven, dedicated himself to the conversion of the Irish race.   After twenty years of training in the school of St. Martin at Tours, he obtained full powers from Pope St. Celestine, was consecrated bishop, and sailed for the Irish coast. The great result of his sixty years' preaching is known throughout the world. He found Ireland heathen, and left it Christian. He encountered the Druids at ·Tara, and abolished their pagan rites. He converted the warrior chiefs and princes, and baptized them, with thousands of their subjects, in the holy wells, which still bear that name. Many youths and maidens embraced the religious state, and schools, convents, and churches rose simultaneously throughout the land. In the midst of this wonderful success St. Patrick's life was, what it had always been, one of penance and prayer, his humility increasing as he drew near his end. Full of works and full of years, the great missionary died at Sabhull, County Down, A.D. 492."

## ST. VERONICA.

On the left, within the altar-rails of St. Patrick's Chapel, is the picture of St. Veronica displaying the Sacred Face. As our Lord was proceeding along the way to Calvary, sinking under the Cross, a woman, moved with compassion, made her way through the crowd, and wiped His Face with her veil. The impression of the Sacred countenance was imprinted on the veil, and the " Sanctum Sudorium " is now among the relics

G

kept at St. Peter's. According to some authors, the name of the Picture—" Vera icon "—" the true likeness," was transferred to the person, who has

ST. VERONICA.

been henceforth designated as Veronica. In any case, the Church guards the veil, as has been said, as a sacred Relic, and the incident forms one of the authorised Stations of the Cross.

*To face p. 99*

THE FONT.

The devotion to the Holy Face has received a new impulse of late through the zeal of Monsieur Dupont, the holy man of Tours, whose process of canonisation is now begun.

Opposite St. Veronica is a votive picture of St. Cecilia, in memory, a Latin inscription informs us, of Cecilia Read, who died in 1882. An invocation of the Saint follows.

## THE BAPTISTERY.

The eastern tower, which is entered from St. Patrick's Chapel by two iron gates, forms the Baptistery, a fine chamber, 15 feet square. The Font is a reproduction in half-scale of that in the Cathedral at Orvieto. The basin is a magnificent block of red African Breccia of octagonal shape. The stem is of Derbyshire alabaster, supported by eight lions of Carrara marble on a base of the same material. A tablet states that the font is a votive offering to the memory of Francis George Goff, who died in 1891.

## THE NAVE AND STATUES.

The spaces between the pilasters round the Nave are occupied by statues of the Twelve Apostles. These statues for some 200 years lined the nave of the Cathedral at Siena, but were removed a few years since, as being unfitted for a Gothic edifice. The figures are of heroic size, in solid blocks of Carrara marble, and were the work of the sculptor Mazzotti, towards the close of the seventeenth century. Most of the figures show the emblems of their martyrdom as traditionally represented in art. The figures of the nave, beginning on the left-hand side on entering, are : St. Bartholomew ; he bears a knife in his hand, as he won his crown by being flayed alive. St. James the Less, the first Bishop of Jerusalem ; he is represented with a book, perhaps significant of the Epistle which bears his name ; at his feet is the Fuller's club, the instrument with which his brains were beaten out by the infuriated populace in front of the Temple of Jerusalem. Entering the western transept, we have St. Philip ; his emblem is a cross with short arms, symbolic either of his martyrdom or his victory over the idols by the power of the Cross. St. John the Evangelist, pen in hand, with

*To face p.* 100.

ST. MATTHEW APOSTLE.

To face p. 101.

ST PAUL APOSTLE.

the eagle at his feet. He is compared with this bird because, says St. Augustine, while the other evangelists walked on earth, he soared above the skies and gazed with steadfast eyes on the light of unchangeable truth. Facing St. John is St. Peter with the keys; "To thee I will give the keys of the Kingdom of Heaven" (Matt. xvi. 18). Within the Sanctuary: St. Andrew, with his diagonal cross. Facing St. Andrew is St. Thomas, with a builder's rule. Under divine inspiration, he offered himself as an architect to Gondoforus, the King of the Indies, to build his palace, and ended by converting the king and his people to the faith. He is the patron saint of architects and builders. In the eastern transept, looking south, are St. Paul, with his book of Epistles in his hand and the sword of his martyrdom at his feet; St. Simon Zelotes the Zealot, with a saw. He was sawn asunder for preaching the Gospel in Persia. Re-entering the nave, St. Matthew, pen in hand, with his Gospel resting on the head of a cherub, admirably executed; St. Jude, or Thaddeus the Brave, with the halberd, the edge turned towards him, the instrument of his passion; St. James the Greater, with a staff, indicative either of his being the first to start on the apostolic mission, or, when the mallet and gourd are added, of him as a pilgrim to Compostella, his own future shrine.

## THE STATIONS OF THE CROSS.

Between the pilasters and above the lower entablature are a series of pictures called the Stations of the Cross, or Via Crucis, because they represent different events in the Passion of Christ. They are fourteen in number, the first being on the left (Gospel) side of the High Altar, the last on the right. They are as follows : I. Jesus condemned by Pilate ; II. Jesus laden with the Cross ; III. His first fall ; IV. His meeting with His Most Holy Mother ; V. Simon of Cyrene bears the Cross with Jesus ; VI. Veronica wipes the face of Jesus ; VII. Jesus falls a second time ; VIII. He consoles the women of Jerusalem ; IX. His third fall ; X. He is stripped of His garments and given gall to drink ; XI. He is nailed to the Cross ; XII. His death ; XIII. The Sacred Body is taken down from the Cross ; XIV. The entombment. The devotion began with the Franciscans, who are the guardians of the Holy Places in Jerusalem, and it is intended as a help to making a pilgrimage in spirit to the scenes of Christ's sufferings and death.

The Stations are performed in procession and with appropriate singing on Friday nights at the Oratory, and are one of the most popular devotions in the Church.

## THE PULPIT.

On the left of the Nave is the Pulpit, a reproduction of that at the Roman Oratory. It is approached

THE PULPIT.

by two flights of steps and contains a chair, as the week-day sermons are delivered seated. Of the style of preaching the rule says, that it is to be simple

and unadorned, and specially suited to the spread
and confirmation of the Faith in England.    In Fr.
Faber's judgment this end was best gained by
teaching Catholic truth in all its branches, the
Dogma of Faith, the Lives of the Saints, the
principles of ascetism, not controversially or with
economy ; but as simply and completely as in a
Catholic land.

On the same principle, the Services and the
popular devotions are to be carried out in every
detail on the Roman model.    Processions with
images and banners, confraternities in their habits,
festoons and lights innumerable, orchestral and
popular music—all that makes a Catholic Feast were
to be found in the Oratory from its opening.

So, too, his hymns with which the services and
sermons are varied and interspersed, expressed night
after night, by the lips and hearts of hundreds, all that
is most tender and touching in devotion, with theo-
logical accuracy of doctrine.    How true Fr. Faber's
judgment was, experience has proved ; what was
thought most hazardous has proved most popular,
and the most crowded nights at the Oratory are
those when the Procession of the Madonna takes
place—that stream of faith which, like the River of
the Psalmist, makes glad the City of God ; or when
the " O Salutaris Hostia " proclaims from a host of
voices that the Eucharistic God is enthroned.

In conclusion, many attempts are being made to educate, elevate, and refine the masses. If prejudice could but be laid aside, if men's eyes could be opened to see things as they are, surely no education can compare with that placed within reach of the poorest by the ritual and surroundings of the Catholic Church. All that sculpture, painting, music, ceremonial can express of what is highest, purest, best, is there—not as a representation of the past, not as a museum of antiquities, or an historical collection, but as voices from Heaven, lifting man from the sorrows and miseries of this life, and quickening him with renewed faith and hope. From the dull and dismal streets of our great city and its begrimed, driven, and melan-

BROTHER OF THE LITTLE ORATORY, WITH BANNER OF THE PRECIOUS BLOOD.

choly population, with nothing to raise their spirits
but a *Bank Holiday*, should the passer-by turn
into the Oratory on any Feast, and see the crowds of
all classes, numbers of the most poor, praising God
with glad voices, or kneeling in silent prayer before
their favourite Altar, or seeking the peace of forgiven
sin in the tribunal of penance, he will understand that
the true remedy for human evils comes only from
above, and that in the desert of this life the Patriarch's vision of Angels ascending and descending
is still seen by the eye of Faith—in that one Sanctuary, which "is no other than the House of God,
and in truth the Gate of Heaven" (Gen. xxviii. 17).

On either side of the Nave are notices inviting
subscriptions for the completion of the Church and
its decorations.   The nave, transepts, and interior
dome  are  still  in  their  unrelieved  whitewash.
Much then has still to be done, but the work will
advance as it has begun—as donors are found who,
like the Magdalen, do what they can, with no thought
of thanks from man, but in gratitude for what God
has done for them.   A Catholic Church should be
what our old Cathedrals were, a complete holocaust of
treasure, genius, and skill offered to the Most High—

CARDINAL NEWMAN'S STATUE.

*To face p.* 107.

a monument of the self-sacrificing devotion of successive generations, each age doing its part, content to leave to posterity the finishing hand.   The House of God is the dwelling-place of the Eternal. It is the fruit not of natural effort, but of divine grace ; and long after its builders are past and gone, its very walls should proclaim, as the old Sequence says, "that they are founded in Faith, raised in Hope, and knit together by Charity."

## CARDINAL NEWMAN'S STATUE.

Facing the Brompton Road on the western side of the Oratory grounds is a statue, erected in 1896 by general subscription, to John Henry, Cardinal Newman.   The design is by Messrs. Bodley and Garner, and was executed by Messrs. Farmer and Brindley.   The figure of the Cardinal in his robes is in Campanello marble, the remainder is in Portland stone and is surmounted by a statue of the Madonna of San Sisto, in the same material.   The Cardinal's history is so well known that we need only note the most prominent events in his career. As the leader of the " Tractarian " movement from 1833 to 1843 ; by his writings in the " Tracts for the Times," the " British Critic," his Sermons, and other works ; by his learning, scholarship ; by his

marvellous English, of which Mr. Gladstone said
that every sentence is a thing of beauty; by his
personal piety and asceticism, he acquired an influence considered by his contemporaries as simply
unparalleled.    According to Professor Shairp, "It
was almost as if some Ambrose or Augustine had
reappeared," and in J. A. Froude's opinion, "all the
rest were but as ciphers, and he the indicating
number."    Being convinced by his study of the
Fathers that "to apprehend the ancient Church as
a fact is to be either a Catholic or an infidel," he
was received into the Catholic Church in 1845.
His secession was described by Lord Beaconsfield,
some years after the event, as "a blow under which
the Church of England still reeled," and Mr. Gladstone has asserted that "it has never yet been
estimated at anything like its full importance."
Besides the foundation of the two Oratories in
London and Birmingham already noted (p. 2), and
the foundation of the Catholic University in Dublin
(1854), of the Oratory School at Edgbaston (1859),
Cardinal Newman's conspicuous works in defence
of Catholicism were his "Discourses to Mixed
Congregations" (1849), the Lectures on Anglican
Difficulties (1850), the Lectures on the Position
of Catholics in England (1851), the latter result-
ing in the Achilli trial, the expenses of which,
amounting to £14,000, were furnished by voluntary

subscriptions at home and abroad.  In 1864, in answer to Kingsley's attack, appeared a detailed defence of his religious opinions in the "Apologia pro vita sua," and in 1874 his letter to the Duke of Norfolk vindicated against Mr. Gladstone's "Vaticanism" the civil allegiance of Catholics. In 1879 Dr. Newman was created Cardinal of the title of St. George in Velabro by Leo XIII., and in the address delivered on his elevation he declared that for fifty years he had resisted to the best of his power the spirit of Liberalism in Religion.*

As a poet, his verses, "Lead Kindly Light," have been adopted as a prayer for faith far and wide outside the Church, while the "Dream of Gerontius," unrivalled both as a text-book for its classic English, and as a drama descriptive of the passage of the soul through death and judgment to Purgatory, has gone through scores of editions.   It has been said with truth that scarce an educated person embraces Catholicism in England, save through the influence, direct or indirect, of Cardinal Newman.

* *Cf.* "Dict. of Nat. Biography," art. Newman.

# INDEX.

BURNS AND OATES, LIMITED, LONDON.